QUEER BODY POWER

of related interest

In Their Shoes
Navigating Non-Binary Life
Jamie Windust
ISBN 978 1 78775 242 9
eISBN 978 1 78775 243 6

Queer Sex
A Trans and Non-Binary Guide to Intimacy,
Pleasure and Relationships
Juno Roche
ISBN 978 1 78592 406 4
eISBN 978 1 78450 770 1

Life Isn't Binary
On Being Both, Beyond, and In-Between
Meg-John Barker and Alex Iantaffi
Foreword by CN Lester
ISBN 978 1 78592 479 8
eISBN 978 1 78450 864 7

Fat and Queer
An Anthology of Queer and Trans Bodies and Lives
Edited by Bruce Owens Grimm, Miguel M. Morales,
and Tiff Joshua TJ Ferentini
ISBN 978 1 78775 506 2
eISBN 978 1 78775 507 9

Queer Body Power

Finding Your Body Positivity

Essie Dennis

Jessica Kingsley Publishers
London and Philadelphia

First published in Great Britain in 2022 by Jessica Kingsley Publishers
An imprint of Hodder & Stoughton Ltd
An Hachette Company

3

Copyright © Essie Dennis 2022

Extract from Butler, J. (2004) *Undoing Gender*. Abingdon: Routledge
is reproduced with kind permission from Taylor & Francis through
the Copyright Clearance Center.

A CIP catalogue record for this title is available from the British
Library and the Library of Congress

ISBN 978 1 78775 904 6
eISBN 978 1 78775 905 3

Printed and bound in Great Britain by Clays Ltd

Jessica Kingsley Publishers' policy is to use papers that are natural,
renewable and recyclable products and made from wood grown
in sustainable forests. The logging and manufacturing processes
are expected to conform to the environmental regulations
of the country of origin.

Jessica Kingsley Publishers
Carmelite House
50 Victoria Embankment
London EC4Y 0DZ

www.jkp.com

For Casey

Contents

Acknowledgements   9

Trigger Warning   11

Introduction   13

In the Beginning, There Was You   25

Reclaiming Your Body   39

Sexuality and Our Bodies   55

Gender Roles? In This Economy?   77

Our Complex Relationship with Food   95

Unlearning Fatphobia   121

Bodies Are Political   137

Social Media and Queer Happiness   157

Saving Ourselves Through Fashion   169

Joyfully Queer Bodies   191

You Are Enough   205

Further Resources   209

References   213

Index   217

Acknowledgements

I would like to thank the people who were interviewed for this book. Thank you for being so open and honest about your experiences.

Molly Elizabeth Agnew

Yasmin Benoit

Stevie Blaine

Kelsey Ellison

Maxine Heron

Jackson King

Amalie Lee

TJ Lucas-Box

James Makings

R.K. Russell

Charl Summers

Mia Violet

Annie Wade-Smith

Trigger Warning

My aim with this book was always to make it helpful and positive. Although trauma and discrimination are mentioned, I have dealt with issues as sensitively as possible. The following list of potential triggers is included, however, so that you can know a little bit about what is mentioned in the book and decide to skip anything that may be triggering for you.

Ableism is mentioned throughout, but there are never any detailed references to ableist violence.

Eating disorders are mentioned throughout, but in the most detail in the chapter 'Our Complex Relationship with Food'. I never go into too much detail but I do talk about disordered behaviour and my mental state during my own recovery.

Fatphobia is mentioned throughout, but in detail in the chapter 'Unlearning Fatphobia'.

Racism is mentioned as an issue throughout, but mostly in the chapter 'Bodies Are Political'. There are references to racism experienced by some of my contributors but there are never any detailed references to racist violence.

Transphobia is mentioned throughout, but mostly in the chapter 'Gender Roles? In This Economy?' There are no detailed references to transphobic violence.

Introduction

What does it mean to be queer? As an activist I find myself thinking about the finer details of queerness – all the little things that make us who we are. Nowadays, it feels like there are two distinct sides of my own life as a queer person. One is the commodified pride. We are loved and valued by the world for one month, for the occasional 'national something day'. Then two, after all that is over, there is the lived reality of queerness. Or perhaps I should say 'the many lived realities'. The reality of feeling strange and wrong for such a long time, trying to navigate a world that has no system for you in all its structures. The reality can be the mental health toll of discrimination, the lack of familial support, the gender dysphoria and the violence we experience. I often find myself pulled between queer joy and queer struggle.

Self-love as a queer person is complex and it has been a reflective journey for me. I grew up thinking that butch was bad, bisexuals were greedy and I shouldn't wear loose clothing because it would hide the curves of my body. Makeup was used for cover, not enjoyment. I was told flowery dresses were flattering (and we all know flattering is code for 'makes you look thinner'), so I wore them. I felt like my body was betraying me, telling the world I was something I just wasn't.

From as young as I can remember, disordered eating blighted my life. Upon much reflection, I realized how intrinsically linked my body image and my queerness had always been: the obsession the world had with how men perceived me, my fertility, my femininity, made me want to shrink my body so I barely existed at all. If I couldn't exist in a way that I felt comfortable, I did not want to take up space. A cultural obsession with thinness convinced me that it must be the fat on my body that made me feel so at odds with everything. Therefore, I began to fixate on my food.

When I was 12 years old, I was diagnosed with anorexia/bulimia. I think perhaps the diagnosis would have been more nuanced nowadays as there were big parts of my eating disorder that were not really noticed, such as intense over-exercising. I mention that this was when I was *diagnosed*, because I would like to make it clear that the behaviour had been there since I was around 6 years old.

I am not the only person who has had experiences with an eating disorder or bad body image as a child, and this makes me wonder just how young body dissatisfaction really begins. I believe that it is woven into the fabric of our personhood from the moment we begin our journey into society, with threads being steadily added over time. Pulling the threads is painful. It feels wrong and unnerving to begin untangling parts of ourselves we thought were so integral: a sense that we are not enough the way we are.

By the age of 16, I was seriously struggling with my mental health. I truly am not being dramatic when I say that being a teenager is a whirling hellscape. Being a queer kid with an eating disorder (attempting to hide both) on top of the early stages of a disability was just awful. And I think when you're that age, you don't necessarily believe that there is a world for you ten years on. I remember clearly thinking that the only way I could possibly be happy was if I lost weight. I struggled a lot with hyperfixation, thinking that complete control over my body would be a cure for sadness. Isn't that what we are always told? Buy this, eat this, drink this, and you will wake up perfect. Capitalism is the puppet master of self-image after all, and it relies on you believing that everything you are is wrong.

I will explain my own experiences more deeply as we move through this book, but it is important for me to show that disordered eating really did shape my adolescence, and recovery shaped my early twenties. Online communities were my saviour. My saviour from wasting away, my saviour from a heterosexual narrative that makes my body squirm.

Though the research is limited, studies have shown that LGBTQ+ people suffer with higher rates of eating disorders than our cishet (cisgender and heterosexual) counterparts (Nagata *et al.* 2019, 2020a, 2020b, 2020c, 2020d). We are more likely to have mental health issues based on minority stress, and this can be based on a broad range of factors: family rejection, public persecution, job loss due to our sexuality and gender. We are shown to have more body dissatisfaction in general. When I learned this, I decided to log into Instagram and post a few questions on my platform. I wanted to know how many of us were suffering and try to see patterns in how people were feeling.

Here are some of the replies I got:

I was overwhelmed.

I'm not thin enough to be androgynous.

I look too feminine to be a lesbian.

I look too masculine to be bi.

I feel like I don't look non-binary enough.

Am I too fat for drag?

I'm worried people won't find me attractive if I am not thin.

I'm worried I'm not muscular enough to fit into gay culture.

I have big boobs so I can't be masculine.

I keep comparing my body to my partner's.

I'm worried my body is not 'queer enough'.

I was struck by how many people repeated versions of that phrase 'I am not enough'.

It was this information that pushed me to consider that our vast community deserves to have resources that address how our position in the world affects our mental health, our body image and our overall self-acceptance. For it is not ourselves that is the problem; it is the way in which the world reacts to us.

This book is a love letter to my community. I want to take everything I have learned from my own experiences and use it to build connections for other queer people. We are so often left out of conversations about body image and mental health, yet it is clear that we suffer more from such pressures than our cishet counterparts do. I wonder if it is because there is not always an understanding of how layered queer experiences are and how much queer identity is intrinsically linked to the politics of bodies. I hope that my own lived experiences will resonate, alongside the contributions of other queer people that I interviewed for this book. I want it to open up a dialogue about queer mental health and body image.

It is not easy to feel like there is not enough space for you in the world or that your body and self-image will never be accepted. I have learned that when it feels like all that is good and easy in the world is not meant for you, you must simply carve out a space for yourself, sit down in it and say, 'I belong.'

A little bit about how I got here

My life as an activist started small. I believe in starting small, in starting with small changes, in constantly building and in constantly changing. Volunteering, fundraising and helping my community are the bedrock of what has always mattered to me. In addition, my enthusiasm for these things was informed by my love of academia and my desire to learn. Learning is a huge part of how I think activism should work. We are always learning and our opinions are constantly becoming more informed. This was why I ended up at university, regardless of the financial struggles that would come afterwards.

However, whilst I was at university, I was forced to confront something that had plagued me my whole life: *my eating disorder*.

I was put in a position where I needed to realize that an eating disorder had really stopped me from living my life the way I wanted to live it. I had been in such an intense state of fear for years. I feared food, and I feared gaining weight and accepting the weight my body wanted to naturally sit at.

I remember one evening, when I was around 21 years old, having a panic attack over how many calories were in a piece of fruit. I was starving. I was sitting at my little student desk, hugging my knees to my chest, looking at the food next to my lecture notes and realizing that I didn't have enough energy to make my brain work. I needed to eat something and yet my mind was screaming at me, 'You can't. What if you put on weight? That is the worst thing that could possibly happen.'

I sit here writing this at the heaviest I have ever been, knowing just how untrue that sentiment was. But I was basically a kid, and I had been told my whole life that being thin, straight and able-bodied were the pinnacles of human existence.

There was something about that moment when I found myself looking at my behaviour, looking at my reaction, and realizing just how absurd it was. It felt absurd. I realized that I had been unhappy for fucking years, and all for what? It was a lightbulb moment and I honestly couldn't figure out why I was clinging so tightly to this intense body obsession when it had done nothing but make me unhappy.

This is not to say that a lightbulb moment equals a quick fix. No. It took me a long time to recover, to unlearn fatphobia, to accept my disability, to come to terms with my queerness. However, this moment was a moment when I realized something needed to change. This was when I decided to make an Instagram account for my recovery.

Mental health support was nearly non-existent for me, as it is for many of us, and I needed to find help on my own. I think that many people have done that, particularly those in recovery, because of a lack of access to therapy and the fear of not being believed.

You can't see this, but I'm glaring down a fake camera at the therapist who told me I was too fat to have an eating disorder when I was 15 years old.

Newsflash: eating disorders are a mental illness and your weight does not define your struggle.

I truly wish that there was more support, particularly for LGBTQ+ people, in terms of eating disorders, and this is a topic I will explore in far more detail in the chapter titled 'Our Complex Relationship with Food'. Luckily, this is something that is being discussed more and more, but when I began recovery, I felt like I had nobody to turn to.

My little Instagram account was just a way of holding myself accountable, and I thought that maybe I could find a community. Well, I did and it changed my life. I found people who had recovered from eating disorders, people who were accepting their weight gain, people with bodies like mine, plus-size fashion bloggers who inspired me, and queer people being open and honest about their experiences. My experience as an online persona is different now than it was at first. When I started, the recovery community was smaller and felt like a safe place that really nurtured my recovery.

As I recovered, gained weight, shared my story and educated myself, my whole outlook on bodies changed. The way we are taught to demonize fat bodies, disabled bodies and queer bodies became more prominent in my mind and I realized why I had been punishing myself for so long.

This also happened to be the same year I came out as bisexual. Do you ever feel like you have all the big revelations in one short space of time? It's like you unlock one box in a pile of boxes labelled 'my authentic self' and decide that you want to open another and then another until everything is out there. I remember talking to my partner about the year they cut their hair, changed their name, came out as non-binary *and* decided to get a massive tattoo across their back. That's sort of how it was for me too. It was another couple of years until I really grew into my queerness, especially my fluid identity, but I think that was the start of me realizing just how much I had to unpack.

I began speaking at schools about body image and queerness, I became more open about living with chronic illness and deteriorating health, I learned more and more about revolutionary histories behind queer liberation. There was a lot that happened in between, and I am sure there is a lot more to come, but the idea of this book really came to me when I was speaking at a particular school event.

I was booked to speak on Body Positivity, and I just happened to mention I was queer during my talk. The response to me being open about being queer prompted a reaction that I hadn't really expected or prepared for. The anonymous responses overwhelmingly included questions about LGBTQ+ issues, alongside questions about body image and eating disorders. Considering how little had been mentioned about queer issues, it was obvious to me that these kids were desperate for more role models, more advice, more understanding and less judgement.

It seemed clear then that LGBTQ+ issues and body image were so intertwined, and yet so much mainstream Body Positivity focused on cishet women. There were often pieces missing from the books I was reading and I found myself yearning for more Body Positive books that focused on queer people and their journeys with their bodies. There were certain experiences I was having in relation to my sexuality, gender and presentation that I hadn't realized affected my body image. Although I did, and still do, relate on some level to the cishet women whose books I read, for my own sanity, I needed more nuance.

They do say you should write the book you want to read.

Queerness is so much more than a label that is supposedly required for dating. It is community, history, how you carry yourself in the world, fluidity, performance, identity, character, heart. Queerness is many things and all of those things at once.

What actually is 'Body Positivity'?

When I talk about Body Positivity, I'm talking about the move-ment itself: the radical act of liberating bodies that have been marginalized by society. Absolutely every human being deserves respect, and it doesn't matter what their body looks like. The reason we need Body Positivity is because certain bodies are treated like they are worth less than others, and that brings up a lot of issues in our society. Although personal body acceptance is a part of it, the movement also recognizes the need for liberation. We have to be honest about the way in which our bodies are treated differently based on gender, sexuality, race, size, disabil-ity and class. There are a multitude of ways in which our bodies are affected by the society we live in and I want this book to go into why queer people need Body Positivity and deserve to feel comfortable in their own bodies. We are too often made to feel like we don't deserve love, respect and human decency if our bodies do not conform to beauty ideals.

You are worthy of companionship regardless of what your body looks like. You are worthy of respect because you are a human being and everyone deserves respect. Queer people are part of this conversation and we have a lot of different experiences in our bodies than cishet people do. I have found myself struggling in many ways, from fatphobia to ableism and homophobia in the workplace, to navigating gender. All of these things have affected my body image.

Body Positivity does not mean that you feel some intense affection for your body at all times. It is not an unattainable goal. It is not toxic positivity, which does not allow us the room to breathe through our pain or address systemic issues. We absolutely need the space to shout at the world, to feel low sometimes, to be angry about how our bodies are treated. We also need the space to be hopeful and optimistic and to focus on personal growth that can lead us to feeling comfortable in our bodies, even in the face of others who might try and bring us down.

I spent a long time trying to construct a suit of armour around myself in order to be protected from the cruelty of those who thought they could criticize my body, my sexuality and my presentation. But that suit of armour was brittle and ultimately useless because inside, I still believed I deserved criticism. I had to accept that if I was really going to feel strong in my selfhood, I needed to accept who I was, and that included the things I had been taught to hate:

My body type.

My disability.

My queerness.

I needed to accept my body for what it was and stop giving people's opinions any space in my reality. Getting to that point seemed like climbing a never-ending mountain.

I want us to write an infinite number of books about this issue, from all different perspectives, because understanding the feeling of isolation that can come from struggling with queerness and body image is something I know I would have benefited from when I was younger. So, if you are reading this book and it brings something out in you that you want to put on paper, do it. I want to read it. I want our community to have more resources.

This book will go into all the different aspects of body acceptance, from both my own perspective and the perspective of other people in the LGBTQ+ community. I am going to delve into the different issues that our community faces in terms of our body image – from eating disorders to gender roles – and I will be very open and honest about my own experiences as a queer person. This book has been written as a push to challenge heteronormative beauty standards, and I also wanted to centre queer people in my own Body Positive discussions. Frankly, I'm sick of the world making us feel inferior because we don't fit into certain boxes. It is easy to internalize all these feelings to the point that you feel like you are inherently not good enough. This book was written to tell you that is not, nor has it ever been, true.

On that note, I want to begin at the most iconic place to start: the beginning. We are going to go into those very first experiences in our bodies and how they lay the foundation for our body image growing up.

In the Beginning, There Was You

Do you remember the first time you became aware of your body? I don't mean being aware that you existed; I mean being aware of your physical body. What moment has become etched into your mind as the moment you realized your body was a form to be appraised and gendered? Looking back, there were two instances of me realizing that my physical form was suddenly up for public consumption.

When I was 7 years old, I realized that the girls in the changing room at school would watch me as I got undressed. They would giggle and raise their eyebrows. It took me a few weeks to properly gauge what the issue was because I hadn't really noticed that bodies were something to focus on until that moment. I knew what women were 'supposed' to look like because I saw the *Vogue* magazines on the coffee table. But I wasn't a woman; I was just a girl.

I went home the first day after it happened and looked in the mirror, noting aspects of my body that I had never scrutinized before. There was one, glaringly obvious, problem in my mind: I was chubby. I look back and think, 'Well, of course I was chubby,

I was 7 years old!' But as a child, I had no concept of body diversity or an understanding of how bodies change and grow. All I knew was that I was wrong and it was my fault.

The second instance was a more insidious one and it brings up the issue of how children are gendered and sexualized against their will. This is an issue for our society as a whole. However, it is all the more potent for queer children who very actively feel alienated by heteronormativity. At 12 years old I was already a few years into puberty and I was struggling with reconciling my body and my identity. As an adult, I now know that my gender presentation is fluid, but back then I did not have the tools to understand that. This left me with a sense of dread as my body changed, because I began to realize that adults were looking at me differently. At the age of 12 I was catcalled in the street for the first time in my life. I can't remember the exact words used – all I remember is an adult man shouting about my breasts at the top of his lungs. After that moment, it felt like adults were commenting on my body left, right and centre, oddly fascinated by the body of a child. I was told I should like my body because I had childbearing hips. I was told I shouldn't feel uncomfortable in my body because men would find me attractive. Defining myself by how much men wanted to sleep with me was pushed on me from an age when I should never have been sexualized in the first place. I was made to feel like any concerns I had about my body and my identity could not exist, because I could easily slot myself into a heteropatriarchal narrative.

But, of course, it's 'the LGBTQ+ community forcing sexuality onto children', right?

What happens when adults – the people you look up to – make you feel that your only worth as a person is through fitting into a certain mould; a mould that you know deep down you can't stay in forever? What happens when you feel like your body is betraying you and signalling to the world you are something you're not?

I liken the feeling of being a queer kid in the closet to being a simmering pot. You try to convince yourself it won't boil over, that you have control over your false image and your false life. You can fit the narrative because the alternative is too frightening. But the pot keeps simmering, then bubbling, and suddenly it's splashing. Your true self eventually boils over because you just can't hold it in any more, nor do you truly want to.

Another question: Do you remember when you first felt the sense of 'wrongness' within yourself? Like there were puzzle pieces within you that you just couldn't jam into place, no matter how hard you tried? I have fragmented memories of feeling uneasy in certain dresses and of a sickly feeling when I fancied girls, realizing what that might mean. I remember adult women I knew being scared they might look butch if they put on weight and had short hair. All the while I was pushing any affinity with masculine presentation as far down as possible.

The truth is, I have always been very fluid:

I liked boys' clothes on some days.

I liked girls' clothes on other days.

I liked doing things that the boys did on some days.

I liked doing things that the girls did on other days.

My body was a strange vessel of confusion as a child. There was such a quick succession of thoughts, from realizing my body existed in the eyes of other people, to realizing everything about it was 'wrong'. *Important note: There is nothing, nor was there ever anything, wrong with you. It is society that has the problem.*

Memories of 'wrongness' are entirely due to a heteropatriarchal world that tries to make sense of you in a way that will never fit.

When they start to put our bodies in boxes

From the moment we are born, we are branded with an 'F' or an 'M': our first marker. Then we are dressed in pink or blue. We are given toys in separate categories. Girls are given little plastic babies to care for and abnormally shaped Barbie dolls to focus on. Boys are given water guns and a licence to be muddy. It is utterly inescapable, right there in black and white: if you're the 'F', your body is for motherhood and desirability; if you're the 'M', then your body is made for strength and wildness. When adults see a girl and boy playing together, they say, 'Ooooh, are you two going to get married?' (Of course you don't want to get married – you're a child.) So, even then, it is made ever so clear that your body is also made for someone else; for marriage to the opposite sex, and ONLY the opposite sex.

There are unavoidable body boundaries from the moment you enter the world. However, LGBTQ+ people have *always* been challenging those boundaries and that is why the nature of queer self-acceptance is so radical.

Throughout history, queer people have explored and expanded concepts of gender, sexuality, bodies, fashion and healthcare. Whilst, as a group, we have a myriad of complex issues regarding our bodies, we also have the power to think and push beyond a heterosexual and patriarchal framework.

Know your power. Know the power in queerness. Know the power that lives within you.

The beginning is always the hardest, and this chapter is about beginnings. At first, you are a child learning to navigate the world through the eyes of adults who don't know how you operate – and perhaps never will. Your body is coded continuously through the misogyny, homophobia, fatphobia and racism around you (we will get to these in later chapters). You are dressed up, told how to be your gender, told how to love and who to marry. There was a beginning when it was just you, but at what point was that taken away? The moment you were gendered? Or the moment you were forced to play with toys you didn't like? Was it when they put you in clothes that didn't feel like you? Or when a family member told you that you were turning into a 'young woman/man'? We all probably have different defining moments in which we felt that surge of 'wrongness' as people defined us in a way that didn't fit.

I decided to ask some LGBTQ+ icons about when they first became aware of feeling uncomfortable in their body.

Growing up in Dallas, Texas, and being Into football, my first questions or discomfort with my body came from the sports world. I wanted to have big muscles, a broad frame, good height, and lengthy limbs. Mine and football's obsession with performance and masculinity drove me to work out, eat a certain way, and continuously disassociate from my own body, viewing it as a tool or product instead of a part of me. This started in my late teens and progressed through my professional football career in the NFL until my late twenties, all while being closeted.

R.K. Russell (he/him)

When I was around 7 years old, I remember feeling sad that I wasn't allowed to do what I wanted with my body. Specifically, I wasn't allowed to wear the clothes I wanted or have my hair in a way I wanted. I was 'stuck' within rules that I didn't agree with. But what I remember more than anything is the strong certainty that there was nothing I could do.

Later, I remember being 11 and realizing that my body was different from the other people my age. I had what I perceived as a giant belly that stuck out in front of me and made me look strange. I started trying to wear clothes that would cover it up.

Mia Violet (she/her)

When I was at a dance competition and somebody said to me about someone else dancing on stage, 'Wow, she's beautiful, she's even skinnier than you!' The tone of their voice made it sound like it was something to be admired, and that's the first time I remember thinking I need to be skinny to look beautiful, not only while dancing but in normal life. It got even worse when I went to Musical Theatre College at 16, where teachers would comment about weight gain and the perfect weight for the stage. I would constantly check my body in the mirror and feel uncomfortable in skin-tight clothes in fear of being assessed.

Kelsey Ellison (she/her)

It started very early on in childhood. I remember crying to my mum, on multiple occasions, that I was fat. That my thighs were too big, etc. This was compounded by comments made by wider family members.

Jackson King (he/him)

The first time I was uncomfortable was when I was getting dressed for PE in Year 6. Back in the day when all the kids would change in the room in front of one another with no inhibitions. Up until then my body was just a tool for climbing trees, playing football and taekwondo. I remember I had some stretchmarks on my stomach and one of the kids shouted, 'Why do you have lots of pink scratches on your body?' It was innocent enough, but then I went on to check the others boys' stomachs and saw no one else had any. I went home and asked my parents, and them being the most lovely and supportive people in the world told me it's completely natural. However, I started to realize that none of the other kids looked like me, so I looked for outside influences to feel like I belonged. I searched media, books and film, and in the 90s let's just say representation wasn't a thing. This left me feeling even more so like my body didn't belong and was the problem.

Stevie Blaine (he/him)

I was diagnosed with scoliosis, which caused my spine to deform into an S shape. At this moment in time I was 14–15. At that age you're just growing into your body, but for me my body was underdeveloping and changing due to my scoliosis. I think at this age, I started to hate a lot of things. One breast was smaller than the other because of my spinal curve. My waist didn't look like the ones on TV. Whilst I couldn't do anything about it prior to my surgery, I started to hide my body and couldn't wait to have it corrected for not only my health, but so my body could look 'normal'.

Charl Summers (she/her)

I remember strongly feeling bigger, both more tall and more fat than my peers, right from primary school. I had to wear women's clothes at a younger age, especially when it came to events like getting a Halloween costume. From this point on, on holidays or at swimming or dancing (wherever my body felt on show or looked at), I would be uncomfortable and felt a lot of shame about the way my body looked. For example, I would cover my belly with my arms until I was in the water or not look in the mirrors at dancing. I spent my teens feeling fat and ugly, and although I was confident in daily life, anything around being attractive or dating I found really hard.

Annie Wade-Smith (she/they)

I remember people at school would always compliment my friends on their looks, then people would stop and say I looked like a boy they knew. One of my friends was very pale, with blue eyes, and was probably a size 6 or less. My other friend was a tall, slender Bahrainian girl who looked like Princess Jasmine. Then there was me. I thought maybe people would treat me better if I had lighter skin, straight hair, a smaller nose, smaller lips – just completely different features – and if I was skinnier. I would Google 'plastic surgery' and imagine the kind of things I might be able to get when I was 18 (not that I ever did). I was actually the same size then as I am now, which is a UK size 8, but my friends were particularly dainty and I felt huge next to them. Then me and my friends started getting social media using our own images, like Facebook, and hanging out with new people outside of our all-girls school. I always remember how I'd post a picture with my friends, and people would only comment on how nice they looked. And when we went out, I specifically remember a boy saying to me when I was 14 that my friend was the pretty one but I had 'great tits'. I started getting more compliments for my body as I got older, almost like people were surprised by my physique, but never got compliments for anything above my chest.

Yasmin Benoit (she/her)

I think generally it was around 12–13 when puberty was on the horizon and my chest started to initially change. That was the moment I knew my 'outside' wasn't matching what I knew it was supposed to be like. When I wasn't allowed to be topless any more as I was 'AFAB' [assigned female at birth], and that was the saddest time for me as a child (in regard to my body and self-image). I remember a specific time (once puberty had happened) where I was on a public bus on the way to school and I had what felt like an 'out-of-body experience' – it felt so real. I visually looked very conforming to what society would deem to be a 'young teenage girl' but I felt the opposite inside and it was like a whole soap scenario happening in my head. This is when I realized 100 per cent something wasn't right and I am not a 'girl'.

TJ Lucas-Box (they/them)

Around age 13, when I realized I wasn't thin. It hit me that I weighed more than the kids around me. I'd see pictures of myself and realize I didn't look like other people did in their pictures. My clothes didn't fit the same, and I wore a size 12–14, and I wasn't very fit or sporty. I realized I didn't see myself as beautiful, or desirable, or attractive. I realized my body wasn't reflected in the media or even the toys I'd grown up with – and that being my size and carrying 'a little extra weight' was only a topic of discussion when seen as a problem to be solved. So, starving myself became my vice in stressful situations (which there were plenty of as a trans kid in my teens).

Maxine Heron (she/her)

I think I'd felt uncomfortable with my body from before I was conscious of it. As a child I was incredibly skinny as I was (and still am) a fussy eater, so people constantly commented on it. Then as I approached secondary school, I gained weight rapidly, and started Year 7 as a chubby kid, so people commented on that too. But I hadn't in any way been mentally prepared for getting bullied for being fat, so it was a really discombobulating time, and I didn't know how to get my head around that to even try to change it. I just knew that my body had never been right, from the outside sources telling me so.

James Makings (he/him)

My discomfort with my body started in my teens. It was not one specific moment, but more a gradually building feeling that eventually manifested in a full-blown eating disorder. To be honest, it was less about my body, and more about my mind. I was in pain, and my body became my punching bag. Needless to say, this punching did not work.

Amalie Lee (she/her)

Those first moments of feeling good

It's easy to focus on the first moments of feeling uncomfortable, because those are the moments that often bring up feelings of inadequacy. However, the first moments of feeling good about your body are also important, even if they are fleeting. This is probably an appropriate time to mention that the word 'good' can mean different things to different people. I don't mean the kind of good you think you feel when you haven't eaten for days and you're looking at a thin stomach the world said you had to waste away for. That is not good. That is another example of trying to force yourself into a box that isn't meant for you. There is sometimes a sense of feeling good about your body when the world starts telling you how amazing you look, but that is not what I mean either. That is still a societal layer, a projection upon you.

This is about feeling good in your body beyond societal context, and it is very difficult to really pinpoint. We are so used to being told how we should feel about our bodies that it is often a long and complex process to unpick how we actually feel. You might never have felt that way, but that's okay because you can and you will.

Even in my adult life, which is so centred around body acceptance, I have found myself asking the question 'Wait, do I actually feel bad about my body right now or is everyone just telling me that is how I should feel?' People genuinely think I should be so upset that I have gained weight in the last few years. People look at me sadly, tell me I have let myself go, and generally assume I must be miserable. So many people could not fathom that I could be happy beyond thinness that there were times I ended up believing it myself.

However, for me, there have been multiple moments in which my brain suddenly clicked and I felt like I was on the right track. I remember going into a clothing shop and for the first time trying on clothes that weren't traditionally sexy. When I say 'traditionally sexy', I mean clothing that suited the male gaze, which both myself and many of my friends at the time all focused on. For most of my teenage years, I felt like I had to conform to a sexuality that was up for cishet male consumption and therefore I wore clothing that I thought would make me look appealing to them. I hated it. To make the conscious choice to go into a shop and buy clothing that fitted my true self was invigorating for a young woman who had yet to engage with the LGBTQ+ community. I saw my body in the formless clothing I'd chosen, feeling a sense of giddiness – as though I could move properly for the first time. There was a sense then that I was slowly taking control, and I know this is a feeling many queer people experience.

I felt a similar way when I realized I no longer hated the cellulite on my legs, something I had been taught to have such an immeasurable disdain for. After so many long years of feeling utterly despondent over the shape and feel of my thighs, I realized one day that I no longer felt that. Sharing my own vulnerability online, my introspection, and the support of a diverse and accepting community helped me feel comfortable with my true self. Accepting your body does not just sit within the confines of looking at yourself naked. It also means enjoying your form, your presentation, your identity. It can sometimes mean neutrality and a distinct lack of feeling uncomfortable. Overcoming my body issue came over time, of course, but it is always important to remember the times we feel positive in our own body image beyond what others tell us to feel.

Different bodies, different experiences

Bodies are encoded with a kind of language. Different bodies are read differently, treated differently, and given different levels of respect and acceptance. Body Positivity cannot exist without fundamentally understanding that certain bodies are afforded different levels of authority in our society.

The LGBTQ+ community is vast and although many of our experiences overlap, they are shaped by our race, class, disability and gender. Throughout this book, I will continue to share the stories of LGBTQ+ people who have different experiences in their bodies from myself, so that both our similarities and our differences can be properly addressed. Intersectionality is key when talking about radical, queer self-love. We all deserve to be represented and to see that our bodies are not bad and wrong. We all deserve to feel safe traversing the world. I suppose the next question that needs answering is: How do we get there?

Reclaiming Your Body

The last chapter focused on those initial moments that we come back to as adults and think, 'Well, that was fucked up, wasn't it?' This chapter focuses on reclaiming your sense of self and reframing the 'supposed to be' about it all. *First things first: your body does not belong to anyone but you.* That might seem like a simple comment. It might seem like an obvious comment. However, there are so many moments in life where our bodies are treated like public property to be commented upon and criticized, it is hard to remember that we don't actually owe anything to anyone. No, you don't owe it to your nan to wear a dress so she doesn't get a shock. No, you don't owe it to your partner to skip your dinner so you stay thin – and while we are on that, if your partner starts body shaming you, you'd better send them packing. No, trans people don't owe it to cis people to conform to gender norms. Most of all, you don't owe it to your community to look a certain way to be considered 'queer enough'.

The world also attempts to use queer bodies as a kind of cultural battleground. Two major cultural moments that have turned queer bodies into political and cultural battlegrounds are the AIDS crisis and the current debates over how much autonomy trans people are allowed over their own bodies. Queer body image is often connected to debates on our identity and right to exist, so our own sense of body acceptance can get lost in the fray. We sit in a political framework we cannot necessarily divorce ourselves from, and our sense of self can become such a battle in itself.

There are consistent fights going on in the public eye – fights that we often have no choice but to take part in because otherwise we could face the loss of our human rights. The term 'minority stress' is thrown around a lot when talking about queer mental health – particularly when we are addressing body image and selfhood. 'Minority stress' refers to the chronically high level of stress that people from stigmatized communities experience, and this kind of stress can mean different things to different people, often worsening when our identity intersects with more than one marginalized community. From my own perspective, being queer, chronically ill and from a working-class background has added a lot of stress to my body image and mental health over the years. When we see our queer selves, in newspapers, on screens, in books and in education, being framed as twisted, insidious, parasitic or the butt of every joke, the fight to love ourselves becomes an uphill struggle. Images of queer people have so long been arbitrated by people who either despise us or do not understand us... How are we supposed to honestly feel about ourselves?

Things that can make us feel really shitty about our body image

These include:

- financial struggles

- lack of an understanding support network

- bullying and harassment from our peers

- lack of appropriate and compassionate healthcare

- pressure to look a certain way from our community

- mental health issues, such as depression, anxiety and eating disorders

- internalized homophobia, transphobia and biphobia

- racism

- fatphobia

- gender dysphoria and body dysmorphia

- feelings of guilt and shame over our sexuality and/or gender.

Sometimes we don't quite know why we are feeling terrible about our bodies. At other times it is very obvious. For those times when you are not quite sure, take a look at everything you are dealing with. Sometimes, the way we feel about our bodies has nothing to do with our bodies themselves but our circumstances, our experiences in our bodies, the weight of the world on our shoulders. We may overlook aspects of our mental health as a contributor to our body image whereas, in fact, our general mental health is a huge influence on our self-image in general.

There are so many good things about being queer. Queer joy is something that has kept me going when everything else is uncertain. But we have to be honest: it can be tough at times and it is the tough feelings we need to work through. Everything can feel so hurtful: like the very air around you is dangerous, like the odds are stacked against you – and sometimes they are. Many of the times I have felt isolated from my body image and my identity have been when my life itself was uprooted.

Those times when my body suffered

A year before I began writing this book, I was homeless. Writing that down gives me a slight jolt. I don't like thinking back, but it matters that I do because I feel no shame. I was not on the streets but I was hopping between different sofas with a backpack whilst I made around £400 a month selling books. Homelessness is a huge issue for young LGBTQ+ people and I knew that I needed to mention it here. Eighteen percent of LGBTQ+ people have experienced homelessness at some point in their lives. LGBTQ+ youth are also more likely to end up homeless than non-LGBTQ+ youth, and 69 per cent are likely to have received familial rejection or abuse (Albert Kennedy Trust 2015). Homelessness can obviously lead to serious issues such as substance abuse, targeted violence and sexual assault, and you can end up in situations that make you feel divorced from your body and your identity.

In terms of my own experience of homelessness, it was not as traumatic as it could have been but it still left me with a sense of fear and sadness that I remember vividly. I was one of the hidden homeless: people who have low-paying jobs and sofas to stay on but are unable to afford a place to live. It is unfortunately becoming a more common occurrence, particularly amongst young LGBTQ+ people.

I don't come from money. I had no safety net. I worked my

way through university. I spent three months relying on the kindness of strangers, wearing the same three pairs of dungarees and absolutely not looking at myself in the mirror. In fact, I remember the first time I did look in the mirror. I can still see it as I close my eyes. Just as I had been rootless and drifting, so had my entire sense of who I was. It was after a long day at work stacking books in the history section of the bookshop where nobody would find me. I took a break and accidentally looked in the little mirror above our staff sink. It felt like the air had been sucked out of me and I was staring at all my emotions laid bare on my skin. My eyes were sunken from stress and I noted the thick, matted mess that was my frazzled, bleached mane of hair. I couldn't remember when I had last brushed it.

Now, I'm afraid this isn't a story about how I saw myself at rock bottom, then had a Mia Thermopolis style makeover and felt fine. It turns out that doesn't actually happen in real life. I can confirm Julie Andrews didn't show up and tell me I was really a princess, either.

Nope, I was still a queer, disabled, working-class 24-year-old looking in a mirror, thinking, 'Well, this is depressing.'

If there is anything I have learned from being involved with Body Positivity online, it is that there is a lot of work to be done – in a personal way and a societal way. Reclaiming your body takes time. It takes bad days, teary days, cheery days, two steps forward, one step back. So on that day, when I looked at myself in the mirror, I went back to the house I was staying in that day and all I did was brush my hair. I was doing one thing to be kind to myself and reconnect to my body after a time of struggle and disconnection.

A couple of years before that, I was finishing my Master's degree. Master's degrees aren't really made for working-class people. I was one of the only students who had to work their way through it, waking up at 5:45 a.m. for my shifts at work, then rushing a few miles to get to my seminars on time. I would then stay on campus until 2 a.m., finishing off the essays I was behind on because I had been working. All the while, I was struggling to afford basic things like tampons and paracetamol and I would sneak some of the wasted food from my shifts at the bakery where I worked and eat it for dinner. Something that very rarely gets spoken about in Body Positive and eating disorder recovery communities is class. I think this illustrates why poverty and lack of resources are a big problem in terms of eating disorders. Food restriction became a necessity at times, which fuelled my negative thoughts about food. I was very fearful that I might end up without the food I needed (I do not believe this would have actually happened, because I had people around me who had proven they would support me in hard times, but that fear was still there).

The stress of being on the edge of broke still lives within my bones.

During that time, I felt like my entire body was deteriorating, like I was utterly bare and vulnerable. I hid my slowly protruding collar bones with high-collared tops so nobody would ask if I was okay. In fact, not long ago I found a photo of myself after an 18-hour day at work, and I felt a pit in my stomach.

My eyes were barely focused, glazed over as though I was existing somewhere else entirely.

It felt like I was.

My final experience of feeling detached from my body is linked to periods of severe illness. I have struggled my entire life with chronic illness but I think when I was young I often pushed through it, even when I was in pain. I was afraid of being seen differently by my peers when I was young – adolescence is already hellish enough. However, there was a point in my adult life when I became completely incapacitated. Very suddenly,

I could hardly walk, my memory was foggy, and I went from being able to move freely to being bedridden. I remember my partner – who at the time I had only just begun dating – taking me for little walks around their house just so I would see the outside in a day. I held onto them so tightly because I knew I might fall at any moment. Disability will be its own topic in this book because it is very integral to my journey of self-acceptance. However, this moment sticks out for me because it was a deterioration of health that happened so drastically I had to re-evaluate how I functioned in the world. Before then, I had managed illness by myself but this was the moment when I really had to accept that I needed help. I hate to say it but I disconnected from my body for a while to cope with the change.

These are not the only times I remember disconnecting from my body but I feel that these ones matter when discussing the kinds of stressors that impact LGBTQ+ people. They were some of the most important times in which I had to reclaim my own identity and my own body.

Healing

During those times, I was so utterly dissociated from my body and I was afraid to focus on it because, if I did, I didn't know what I would find. I knew I felt ill but I pushed myself to my limit just to survive, and there was so little room for self-love or self-care.

At least, I *felt* like there was no room for self-love or self-care. I was wrong about that. No matter what, there is always space for kindness and self-soothing. There is a societal expectation that we can only be kind to ourselves when we are happy, when we are no longer struggling, when we are successful by a capitalist metric; that perhaps we just don't deserve a break from self-criticism or self-hatred, because we are not yet palatable enough. Maybe if we find a way to assimilate into an upper-middle-class, white, cishet paradigm, we can start having bubble baths, eating tasty food and treating ourselves, but not yet. 'Right now, the outside world is too harsh and cruel,' I would think. 'I just need to get through it, then I can breathe again.'

No.

That is not a way to exist. Neglecting self-care and self-love when you are struggling is like telling your best friend to fuck off when they come to you crying. Those times of being disconnected from my body were unsustainable because I was neglecting so many forms of self-care – right down to my nutrition – and I eventually had to slowly build myself back up. That disconnection forced me to build up habits again over time, from concerted efforts to brush my hair to washing my body thoroughly. Sometimes you reach those low moments only to learn that there is a different way of doing things.

I realized that it was vital to my survival that I begin engaging with my body in a kind way. I had to be kind, no matter how my body looked, no matter how much it changed, no matter how other people perceived me. It was my responsibility to make peace with my body after neglecting my own wellbeing for so long.

Self-care is more than just buying things – trust me

As much as I joke about self-care being bubble baths and treating yourself, it isn't that. Of course, it can be if you have the means, but I didn't spend this whole chapter so far talking about the struggles of being working class and queer to just end up telling you to buy things for your mental health. During the most difficult times for my body, self-care was the little things, the things that we don't always do when we are punishing ourselves:

· Making sure you brush your teeth.

· Having a bath or a shower.

· Making your bed.

· Airing out your room.

· Eating food you enjoy.

· Wearing clothes or makeup that make you feel comfortable/euphoric, whether in private or public.

· Connecting to queer people, online or in person. Seeking community is so important.

· Engaging with hobbies that are separate from your body (if you are struggling with focusing on your body). My favourite thing to do is draw.

· Establishing your boundaries and putting them in place. When I'm struggling with my mental health, I will be very honest with people and tell them I cannot communicate with them at that time but I still appreciate them.

· Prioritizing your health as much as you can, whether that means going to see your GP or reordering the meds that you have been putting on the back-burner.

Look, I'm neurodivergent and I am a supreme list maker. This also makes me a good scrapbooker (another fantastic hobby). It felt natural to make a self-care list here because it is the mundane things we need to do for our bodies that we sometimes forget. Having an expensive bubble bath doesn't necessarily help as much as making sure you have enough antidepressants to last you the month, you know? I say this from my own perspective as someone who spent about nine months buying bath bombs before finally realizing I needed some serotonin. Self-care can just mean taking control of certain aspects of your life that maybe you have felt disconnected from, including your body.

Reflect, reflect, reflect

Self-reflection is something I mention often in my everyday life. It is hugely important to learn to grow as a person by being honest with yourself about why you are struggling. Sometimes self-reflection is hard because you might feel uncomfortable with who you see in that reflection, but it is better to be honest with yourself than to punish yourself.

These are the ways I learned to reflect on my selfhood and reclaim my body:

- Realizing that everything I have ever been told about what my body means is a construct and I can take that construct into my own hands. I have more power than I realize.

- Just because some people think that the way my body looks is a signifier for who I am, it doesn't mean they are right. People have told me for years that the fact I have big boobs means I'm somehow inherently hyperfeminine and sexual. As a fluid-presenting person who is on the asexual spectrum, this felt violating. I began to challenge myself: my breasts are just breasts. They're just a part of my body and have no bearing on my selfhood. What other people think about who I am is irrelevant. I know who I am, deep down. The way my body is coded by others has nothing to do with who I actually am, because they don't live as me.

- Self-reflecting on my own body fears. For instance, why am I afraid of looking *too* curvy? Is it because I was sexualized too young? Or is it because my body has been coded as ready to bear children when I don't actually want them? Why am I afraid of gaining weight? Am I worried about how people will treat me? Is my identity too attached to the idea of thinness? It is okay to ask yourself questions, even if you don't have an answer straight away.

- Focusing on euphoric experiences with my body to help guide me in the direction to acceptance. The easiest way I have found to do this is through experimenting with fashion and figuring out what I like without focusing on the societal expectations of my body. The concept 'if it feels right, it probably is' applies here. Beyond expectations for your body that have been hammered into you from a young age, what actually makes you happy? It is all about getting to the core of what fills you with a sense of joy.

- Being open and vulnerable with others – especially queer people. More often than not, we are all feeling the same way but we just don't always feel comfortable expressing it. Some of the most impactful moments in my life have been when I shared my doubts, fears and uncertainties with others who understand. 'Chosen family' exists for a reason.

Learning how to reframe your experiences in your body will not necessarily be an overnight 'fix' but it has allowed me, at least, to be kinder to myself. The media is not always kind to queer bodies. Our family are not always kind to queer bodies. We are not always kind to our own bodies. However, we can learn to be kind. Body dissatisfaction does not have to be the norm.

Speaking with other queer people for this book was hugely important and I wanted to hear about how they cultivated their body confidence. It is different for everyone, but a positive thing for me was hearing from others that it is possible to feel comfortable and happy in yourself, even if it isn't the case all the time. I asked them, 'What makes you feel confident in your body image and self-expression?' This is what they had to say.

> I think it's just being able to look at myself in the mirror and think that I look badass. Once I got away from my school bullies and the people who caused me anxiety, a lot of things improved for me mentally, and I went back to just caring about pleasing myself – which was my mentality as a kid. I subconsciously try to emulate the powerful women I saw growing up who I thought looked really cool, whether it be female wrestlers, or video game characters, or musicians. When I feel like I'm transmitting that same energy and that I look like someone my younger self would think was cool, I feel confident.
>
> Yasmin Benoit (she/her)

> I think I'm lucky in that I'm a pretty positive person. I tend to look at the good over the bad, and can always find some light in the darkness. That has stopped me from being too hard on myself about my body as I've got older, and made it easier for me to look at my body in a positive light. I also find taking and sharing pictures on Instagram really helpful for maintaining a positive image of my own body, because I am in control of the

narrative. I can express my creativity and project how I want people to see me, whilst maintaining honesty about who I am. I also get messages from people – especially gay men – on a daily basis, saying how what I post helps them accept their own bodies, and that always helps me feel confident.

James Makings (he/him)

The biggest factor is avoiding scales and making sure to celebrate my beauty on a regular basis – I will literally chant to myself on my way to work that I'm fabulous and capable and strong and beautiful and independent of any insecurities. I try to focus on being rich in experiences, and therefore rich in life.

Maxine Heron (she/her)

I feel most confident in my body when it performs, whether that be hitting a new high in the gym, becoming more flexible with yoga, sleeping sounder, or waking up early without being groggy. I want to serve my body, fuel it right, rest it, stretch it, pamper it; and in return, it serves me when I need it, and I feel most confident in this sacred exchange between us.

R.K. Russell (he/him)

It's being in a place where I don't even think about the parts of me I spent years hiding under layers of clothes. It's not crying when someone uploads a picture of me showing my visible belly and man boobs. It's embracing all that I am, breaking down outdated male tropes and looking fab whilst doing it.

Stevie Blaine (he/him)

Today, selfies are one of the most powerful tools for helping me feel confident. There's something very empowering about taking a photo of myself and then being in full control of what

I do with it. Normally I have no control of how people see me, but a selfie gives me that control back and also affirms that it's my choice to be seen. A selfie is the most authentic and grounded way for me to say to the world, 'Here I am, I'm happy, this is me, and I wanted to share myself with you.'

Mia Violet (she/her)

Feeling confident in my body has taken years of work and growth. Coming out when I was 16 changed the game for me. I was no longer hiding this integral part of my identity and so I felt I had the freedom to express other parts of my identity too. The way I dress and the clothes I choose to wear have a great impact on my self-confidence too. Social media can often be a dark place, and can certainly bring down one's confidence in one's body image, but for me, it has actually been beneficial. Seeking out influencers and models with similar bodies to me gave me more confidence in mine.

Molly Elizabeth Agnew (she/her)

More so recently, I have found a new lease of confidence in finally purchasing clothes that I like without a care of what others may think. It may seem a simple task; however, I have lived a life conforming to society's standards, so this outbreak has allowed me to explore what I think looks good on my body.

Charl Summers (she/her)

There are lots of ways in which we can cultivate our own sense of peace with our bodies, even in the face of a world that is trying to twist us into something we are not.

Here are some of the ways I very actively challenge negative feelings about my body:

- I challenge negative thoughts when they happen, and replace them with something positive, even if I don't truly feel that way. Even saying positive things to yourself in the mirror when you don't believe them at first can be helpful.

- I wear clothes that are easy for the senses: particularly touch. Clothes aren't all about how they look, and clothes that feel comfortable on your skin help you feel more settled in your skin.

- I stopped comparing my current body with previous versions of my body. I have been known to look back on younger photos and feel like I had 'lost' my body. Nobody loses their body – our bodies just change. It is the most natural thing in the world and it is important to focus on accepting that.

- I learned to call people out when they commented on my body. What this really did was allow me to start outwardly respecting myself, rather than apologizing for myself. Oh, I put on weight? So what?

- I worked on no longer body checking. Body checking refers to the close monitoring of your body, which can manifest in things like excessive measuring or consistent focus on small perceived 'flaws'. If I have a bad moment with my body image and I know I am about to start fixating on my body, I will very actively make sure I focus on something different for the day and stay away from mirrors. This is not necessarily because I dislike my body, but sometimes it is a good idea to stop centring your body on days when you are struggling.

However, there are also outside matters at play that we need the space to talk about. I have made peace with being chronically ill, for instance, but many people around me have not, and that adds an extra pressure to my experience in my body. Although body confidence may often be framed solely as a personal journey, it cannot be entirely placed upon the individual. We all have very different journeys when it comes to accepting our own bodies, and nothing exists in a vacuum.

One huge factor affecting queer people's body image and mental health is sexual orientation. Coming out and accepting our sexuality can often be messy and confusing and can bring up a lot of emotions. I didn't quite realize just how much accepting my sexuality allowed me to reflect on why I had been punishing my body – from my experience of sex itself to the pressure on my mental health – and that is something that requires open, honest discussion.

Let's go deeper into the web of sexuality and our body image.

Sexuality and Our Bodies

For so long, I thought that my own sexual orientation had everything to do with who I wanted to have sex with and nothing to do with who I was as a person. In my head, it was to do with my relationship to others rather than the core of my being. I think this had a lot to do with how queerness was talked about throughout my life – always that vulgar, oversexualized caricature that homophobes create, with very little humanity. This sense that my sexual orientation was only relevant to who I was intimate with led me to feel like I had no culture to engage with, that queer people were nothing more than their romantic relationships. There were a lot of baby steps I had to take to fully realize our history, our fashion, our culture, our struggles, our beauty.

I now see my queerness as an integral part of my being, something that exists regardless of who I am sleeping with or in a relationship with. There is a lot of talk around the idea that our queerness only exists in relation to others, rather than being a part of who we are. This idea perpetuates the erasure of many sexualities, such as bisexuality and pansexuality, and also of people who are asexual and aromantic. It also makes it very difficult for people who are yet to have any kind of sexual or romantic relationship to feel like they belong in the community.

Your queerness is defined by you. It can be as fluid or as rigid as you like. What is meaningful to you may not be to someone else – and vice versa – but your queerness is no less valid or real. In this chapter, I really want to focus on how coming to terms with my sexuality helped me become more at peace with my body, and why that was. At the root of it, feeling at peace with your identity is a key component in feeling more comfortable with your body and there are many factors to that.

Sometimes, we are born and raised in places that do not allow us to express ourselves properly. We may be unsafe or we may be in denial. There are many reasons why coming out – or rather, inviting people in – can be a difficult experience. When you are concealing a certain side of yourself, your exterior can feel even more important. How should I dress to hide this? How should I behave to hide this? Everyone else looks like this – should I look like this too? Why don't I feel comfortable in my body?

I wish I had known when I was younger just how much euphoria I could feel in my own skin and not 'after I lost weight' or 'after I could afford better clothes'. I owe a lot to the queer people in my life for giving me space to accept my sexuality and, in turn, accept my body and my place in the world.

Coming out, then coming out again...and again

The process of 'coming out' is ongoing. The visibility of your queerness is different in different places and you are often pushed to come out over and over again, depending on where you are and who you are speaking to. I still find myself coming out on a regular basis, wondering when it might be the right time to do so or how someone might see me differently, and stumbling over the right words to use.

There are two main prongs to my sexuality and this is because I am both bisexual and on the asexual spectrum. There are therefore two different levels of explanation I have to go through with both of those identities and it can become exhausting. 'Queer' is an easier term for me these days, but both of those identities still have an effect on how I experience my body.

As a bisexual person, I have struggled with feeling erased by cishet people and queer people alike. Even though I came to realize I'm not particularly interested in men, my previous relationships with men were coded as straight and that just cemented this idea in me that my sexuality was dependent on who I was with. That is why it took me a long time to unlearn the idea that my identity was intrinsically linked to my partner at any given time. Because bisexual people are often treated as though their attraction is 50:50 between the two binary genders, this also meant that I was not able to reflect on the fact that my sexuality was heavily skewed towards women or that it was extremely fluid. My life had been so rigidly structured by heterosexuality, particularly my sense of success, that I ignored the very obvious fact that I had feelings for women throughout my life. It felt like I was living through a haze for years, always feeling slightly uneasy that I couldn't see any future five feet in front of me. When I came out to myself, I could suddenly see the path I had been searching for my whole life.

However, once I came out, I began to feel a level of pressure I hadn't felt before. I felt that I wasn't allowed to take up a certain amount of space, because I didn't look 'queer enough' or act 'queer enough' – a concept which none of us can define yet seems to plague many conversations about queerness. I do not think that this is a feeling limited to bisexual people; many queer people are put in a position where they feel they have to prove their sexuality. We end up putting walls up around ourselves that don't give us the option of exploring our queerness. From my own perspective, I often felt locked out of exploring things such as fluid presentation, queer expression and body acceptance through the lens of queer femmes. These are some of the most significant things for me now.

Another side of coming out is coming to terms with being on the asexual spectrum. The intense oversexualization of women, particularly queer women, from a heteropatriarchal perspective, has often put me at war with my body. I started to understand that my feelings around being sexualized against my will, alongside being uncomfortable with many sexual situations, contributed to my feeling like I had no agency over my body. It felt that, no matter what I did, I would be seen as a hypersexual being, when in fact, the opposite was true.

Both initial 'coming out' moments for me were quiet and with the partner I was with at the time. I always had close relationships with partners, and the reason I often describe it as 'inviting people in' is because that was always how it felt. A friend of mine once described it as that and it stuck with me for years. I am inviting you to see a part of me you did not see before, I am inviting you to know me better and support me, I am inviting you to see my authentic self. Telling just one person felt like the first step on the road to allowing myself the opportunity to be openly queer, to be honest about what my body and presentation meant to me.

Alongside the positive aspects of coming out, there are also the negative aspects. Many of us struggle with the expectations of how LGBTQ+ people should look, and coming out can feel like exploring a new territory.

I must admit, some people I know have flourished after coming out, some have struggled immensely and, often, people have experienced a mixture of both. I want to be honest in this book about my own difficulties with fully exploring my own sexuality, because there have been many. Even if we aren't of the same sexual orientation or gender, I know commonality can be found in many queer experiences. I really struggled with feeling like I had to hit the targets of what a queer woman looked like and what my body had to look like to hit those targets.

Some of the thoughts that ran through my head were:

Will girls find me pretty?

Will I be welcome in queer spaces if I don't look 'queer enough'?

Do I need to be thin to explore masculinity?

I want to change my look, but what will my authentic self mean to others? How will people react?

I don't know what I'm doing.

I had this urge within me to reappraise myself, to figure out what I actually wanted to look like. I think for a long time I kept seeing my weight as the issue that was keeping me from some kind of 'true self', but I came to realize that actually it wasn't that. It was a much bigger identity issue that I tried to hide through weight control. Embracing queerness gave me the opportunity to explore the idea that I didn't need to conform to a heterosexual idea of what to look like.

Different communities hold different aesthetic standards, and my own experiences have been from within groups of queer women and femme, non-binary people. That is my personal perspective, which is interesting because activism related to queer women in particular has a very solid foundation within the Body Positivity movement. Feminist theory and criticism have been challenging the way women's bodies are coded for years, unpicking the way in which patriarchal values label, confine and ultimately control women's bodies. I have found myself having really positive and eye-opening discussions with queer women and non-binary people about my body image and those have always outweighed the negative ones.

However, many queer men I have spoken to seem to have dealt with more overt body shaming from other queer men, something that is backed up in lots of different research I will reference throughout this book (for example, Rawlings 2016). In itself, that is an issue to be discussed, and it is helpful that we at least have some data on body dissatisfaction among cis gay men. And, although much of the research is cis-focused, my conversations and interviews with trans men and trans masculine people have shown that the pressure to look a certain way absolutely affects them too.

Don't worry, there will be an entire chapter on gender coming up where we can get into the nitty-gritty of how our gender identity specifically affects our body image.

However, for now I want to share my own stories alongside the stories of other queer people about how our sexuality shaped our body image.

Re-evaluating heterosexuality

The idea of heterosexuality is specific. We are essentially sold an idea of how heterosexuality functions, how we are supposed to behave, feel, live and present. Even people who are not queer are subject to the strict rules that our society has put in place in terms of our sexuality, and it can be extremely stifling. The creation of a Western society that claims heterosexuality is the only way for humans to function comes from the ghost of imperialism (Chang 2014). Across the world and throughout history, our definition of queerness has not been treated as though it is depraved or unnatural, but many countries in the world continue to experience the repercussions of things such as imperialist anti-sodomy laws (Chang 2014).

One of the wonderful things about queerness from my own perspective is that it opened the doors to different ways of being and expressing myself. Overall, I have always found a push to reject what a heterosexual culture has told us creates our value.

What was my value?

My attractiveness to cishet men. The roundness of my hips. My breasts. My ability to bear children. A type of femininity that I didn't quite gel with and couldn't engage with authentically.

I spoke with Maxine Heron about seeking validation via heteronormative standards and trying to unlearn how queer women in particular have been taught to view themselves.

Seeing myself as a whole person, and not just a woman desired by men, is a never-ending project. It's a bizarre cycle. Objectively, I realize I have a lot to offer, but seeking validation in cishet men has been a tough habit to break. 'Maybe it's okay that I'm trans, because he's not afraid to love me/be with me/ sleep with me/tell his friends about me.' It's something that's very tricky to navigate in my dating life and my codependent tendencies – I have a history of putting my entire self-worth in whether or not the person I'm with is seeing me how I'd like them to see me. It's made my relationships exhausting. Over the last two years since coming out as trans, the only comments that have bothered me from trans exclusionary radicalists are those claiming that I am perpetuating misogynistic beauty norms and reinforcing the gender binary which already oppresses women, without trans women contributing to this. Of course, I wholeheartedly disagree with them. I am me, and I am valid, because I say so. But I look in the mirror at my long hair and my makeup and my flattering clothes and (occasionally) my heels, and I try to tell myself that I'm not pandering to these norms. I am wanted by men, and separating myself from that – moving away from any power or value held within that desire – is tricky.

Maxine Heron (she/her)

Separating ourselves from the pressures of heteronormativity is difficult – particularly when the wants and needs of cishet men are put above everything else. We also need to re-evaluate how we define ourselves by the people we are with and how our sexuality impacts our sense of self.

Our bodies are prescribed value based on cisnormative, heterosexual factors, and when we start to change that and show others that we don't have to correspond to those values, we are treated like traitors. In a way, I suppose we are.

In the previous chapter, I spoke about how our bodies become political battlegrounds, and that is very much linked to sex and relationships. In terms of sexual orientation, a narrative was created around the AIDS crisis that still affects queer people today. These ideas of contamination through our sexuality that were peddled via media outlets really continue, and images of the declining health of gay and bi men in particular have a lasting impact (Chapman 1998). The AIDS crisis is just one cultural moment that meant queer sex and relationships have been demonized and pathologized.

There is also a stereotype that follows both queer cis women and trans women: that we are somehow predators. This rhetoric is attached to trans women even more than to queer cis women and is indicative of a culture that oversexualizes queer people and therefore treats us as though we will sexually harass heterosexual women by default. In our current climate, a lot of this is aimed at trans women and the language used is reminiscent of ways in which queer people have regularly been coded as morally corrupt.

It is not easy to live under such scrutiny and have your body thrust to the forefront of every conceivable criticism. It is not easy to be oversexualized in a way that erases your humanity and frames you as a villain.

Re-evaluating heterosexuality and how it imposes standards on what we do with our bodies does not just apply to queer people who feel romantic and sexual attraction, but also to those who don't. There are lots of expectations when it comes to sex and our bodies. There are expectations about how often we have sex, how much we owe sex to others – which we absolutely do not, let me say – and the manner in which we have it. There is a huge misconception around how aromantic and asexual people present and experience their bodies.

I spoke with Yasmin Benoit about some of these misconceptions.

There's a strange belief that if you're not sexually attracted to anyone, then you should be sexually unattractive (which isn't always within your control); you just need to do everything you can to be unappealing and not attract attention, otherwise – especially as a woman – you're a cock tease who is giving off mixed signals. The media stereotypes people who don't experience sexual attraction (or at least, they don't seem to) as being quite nerdy or square (think Sheldon Cooper), or at least homely and plain, inoffensive. We're often depicted as white, which adds another layer to the way Black asexual people are perceived in a culture that hypersexualizes us. But you can be asexual and hot and look like a freaking rock star if you want to. I think confidence has a lot to do with whether other people think you're attractive or not, and it plays a role in the idea that asexual people are meant to be shy, insecure, and make themselves smaller. I want to help empower asexual people to feel like they can express themselves however they want to and show non-asexual people how diverse the asexual community is.

Yasmin Benoit (she/her)

It was really important for me to be able to discuss and write about how asexuals are perceived because – as someone who is on the asexual spectrum – I definitely struggled to understand why my body was being hypersexualized. It always felt very alien to me and it wasn't until I started to accept my queerness that I felt like I took control of the narrative around my body.

Re-evaluating heterosexuality also helped me become more sex positive and in tune with what my body actually wanted and needed. Sex-positive spaces are so important for our body image, particularly when the dominant narrative around queer sex can be so damaging.

Let's be clear:

There is nothing wrong with having lots of sex.

There is nothing wrong with having no sex.

It is your body and therefore, your rules.

Queer sex is still sex.

Exploring sexuality and feeling comfortable in what you want or don't want is a normal thing to do and we are so often shamed for that. We are told that we have to stay within a very particular set of parameters when it comes to sex and relationships, and that can put us in positions we don't want to be in. It can be really difficult for our self-image if we are not being true to what we want out of sex.

All of this feeds into a lot of internalized shame, which really hinders us from being able to explore our queerness and our bodies in an authentic way, free from judgement. This is why we need safe, queer spaces in which to discuss our bodies and our sexuality.

How my sexuality informed my body acceptance

I like the word 'bisexual'. It is a word that feels right to me. It feels cosy and warm and authentic to me. However, I am a very fluid person and I'm happy just identifying as 'queer'. For me, the label was really important when I first came out and I think that was because I hid my queerness for so long, I finally wanted to be very open about it. I liked feeling secure in a label after the insecurity that comes from hiding. I spent years trying to figure out exactly what my sexuality was, treating it like it had to be a fixed point and I needed to prove it to the world. I came up against a lot of gatekeeping, lots of people trying to define my queerness for me, demanding to know how many women I'd slept with, as though if I hadn't slept with enough, then they would revoke my Queer™ membership card.

Coming to terms with my queerness made me realize why I had struggled so much with my body and presentation growing up, and my acceptance of that side of myself allowed me to heal.

I had feelings for girls from around the age of 10. I remember some of my first crushes and I particularly remember that my body insecurity was often rooted in my worry that I would not be deemed good enough for girls to like me. I was much more preoccupied with how girls would perceive me than boys – that still stands, honestly – but I also began to experience a sense of shame that I felt the way I did towards them.

There is a common feeling among sapphic people where you feel slightly predatory for being interested in girls. I think that comes from a lot of deep-rooted homophobia which perpetuates the idea that queer attraction is depraved. This feeling created an idea in me that I had to shield myself from engaging with women's bodies, that there was something wrong with me and my love and admiration of women's bodies was absolutely not allowed.

I struggled with the very concept of touching other girls, which is why, growing up, I would barely hug my female friends. I think I wanted to hide from that part of myself that was curious about being attracted to girls. I also remember very vividly feeling a yearning to be more masculine and I was fascinated by the idea that there was a bigger world of options out there for me – beyond all the clothes I hated and the boys I didn't really like but whose attention I was convinced was my only goal as a girl.

Competition is often pushed upon children who are assigned the same gender, and I felt this very strongly growing up. Competition between girls is framed in the context of beauty and our ability to attract men – personalities or skills be damned. I remember quite vividly feeling an odd mixture of emotions towards girls as I became a teenager. I was afraid of any positive emotional feelings I had towards them in case they developed into something more. I found myself fixating on the fact that my body was different to the other girls and convinced myself that I wanted to just be like them, emulate them, somehow turn into them. At that age, I found that prettiness was important to me in a way it absolutely isn't now. I struggled with having female friends because, as much as I wanted them, I felt that I wasn't good enough to be around them. Underneath that was an intense fear of having to admit that I was queer. I think I was just afraid of rejection for who I really was.

There was very little queer representation around me growing up. Diversity in representation matters because you are able to not only see yourself but see the infinite possibilities in queerness. I really wasn't given the tools to be able to explore who I wanted to be and understand that, yes, my body was a queer body, and just because my body was fetishized by heterosexual men, that didn't mean that I was what they wanted me to be. I really ended up believing that no woman could ever find me attractive, could ever fancy me, could ever love me or even like me. I thought that my bodily worth was solely in the eyes of cishet men, whom I didn't really have much in common with usually. Somehow, I had been taught over time to think that:

- women were my competition and we were incapable of having any meaningful affection for one another

- what cishet men thought about me and wanted from my body defined my worth

- women could not possibly be attracted to me because I was chubby, had dark body hair and cellulite.

That last one still gets to me. My own experience as an adult with queer women has been one of acceptance when it comes to my body. However, whilst growing up I think I projected my own hatred towards my body onto other people and assumed they felt the same way. I was bullied quite relentlessly over my body type and I know that had a negative effect on my self-esteem. That took me to a place where I just assumed that everyone hated my body like I did, unless they were fetishizing me. However, that wasn't and isn't the case. A few bullies can get into your head and make you think every person you come across feels the way they do, and you start to feel insecure about the very way you move. Sometimes I wonder about all the other queer girls at school who were probably feeling exactly the same way I was and never said a word.

It took quite a long time to unpack my feelings towards my sexuality and my body. When I came out at 21, I didn't have the queer community around me like I do now, and I think I was still completely sure that I had no place within it. Everything was a slow process: slowly seeing more people around me come out, slowly seeing more queer people on my social media, slowly having more queer people around me who showed me their multitudes so I felt comfortable exploring mine.

Learning more and more about queer history also helped me immensely. I began to see myself in people throughout history, I saw how I wanted to present, I saw how I wanted my relationships to be. Getting older and more informed meant that I slowly felt more and more like a whole person who didn't necessarily have to spend their entire life performing.

I didn't have to perform a bastardized version of myself forever.

A lot of my own personal body acceptance came from accepting my sexuality. The two are intrinsically linked for me. Picking yourself apart and trying to understand who you really are means that you also have to come to terms with who you really are. I used to dream of being someone else, someone in an easier body than mine. Someone thin, blonde and able-bodied.

I hoped desperately that I could become that. But I couldn't. Embracing who I actually am meant embracing parts of myself that I spent a long time hating, including my body, including my sexuality. When I began accepting my love for other women, I stopped being so intensely critical of women's bodies, including my own. Seeing the body diversity among queer women made me feel euphoric.

Seeing queer, fat women who were super-androgynous and didn't give a fuck?

Bliss.

Finding the bodies of other chubby women attractive and that being a positive thing?

Double bliss.

Not all of our journeys are the same and I don't know how my experience would have been different if I was out younger or had a queer community around me earlier. Although coming out as an adult was initially difficult because I felt like I had spent so much time living a lie, I think I had the tools to deal with it and accept myself more fully. I was already part of Body Positive communities, I was already unpacking my feelings towards my body, and accepting my sexuality felt like the piece of the puzzle that just slotted in perfectly and started glowing magically.

I think we don't always realize just how much of how we were socialized needs to be challenged and how much that corresponds to how we feel about our bodies. It takes work, but that time is well spent because it makes you stronger in your own identity. I spend a huge portion of my life being body shamed online and there was a time when that would have crushed me. But now? I genuinely like who I am and, regardless of my insecurities, that will always stand true.

Some of my tips from my own experience of understanding and accepting my identity are:

- Don't put limits on what you think queerness is, because what you are really doing is limiting your own opportunity to explore your identity.

- Labels are great, but there is no rush to settle on one. You also have every right to change your labels the way you see fit.

- If you are worrying that you don't look like other queer people, then seek out diverse queer media. Putting effort into finding diverse queer bodies truly made me feel so much more comfortable accepting myself.

- Make sure you don't get sucked into valuing yourself through other people's eyes. Lots of people, especially people you have known for a long time, might code you in a way that isn't you. Your identity is not theirs to cultivate.

- When you are feeling bad about your body and your sexuality, take a minute to sit with yourself away from the mirror. It is easy to lose ourselves in the mirror when we feel low, and grounding myself in how I felt rather than how I looked was helpful when I needed to challenge my own lack of self-worth.

Fear of ageing is detrimental to the LGBTQ+ community

Do you ever feel like you are living your teenage years a little late? I didn't realize I felt that way until I met my partner. Even though they came out as a teenager and I came out as an adult, neither of us could really embrace our queerness openly until we were older. When you are straight, you are allowed to explore your identity, sexuality and body as a teenager – in fact, it is considered completely normal to do so. However, when you are queer, there are barriers to that. Hopefully, this will not be the case forever, but certainly for my generation – as a millennial – there was a big chunk of childhood where we couldn't ever talk about queerness at school. Even now, being openly LGBTQ+ as a teenager is really challenging. This makes a lot of the ageism in the LGBTQ+ community even more of an issue, because many of us are expressing ourselves the way our younger selves would have when we are older. Those pivotal experiences of coming to understand yourself and your identity, breaching the world of dating, finding your own style, are all things that queer people are not always able to do as young people.

In our community there is certainly a cultural obsession with ageing and the privileging of youthful bodies. There is also a lot of trauma around ageing in our community, from losing so many young queer people to AIDS to the mental health of older LGBTQ+ people being largely ignored. Trans people are also not necessarily given the opportunity to safely transition until they are older, which means that a cultural focus on age makes being able to transition later in life seem less important. It's not. In the media, older queer bodies and older queer love and affection are rarely shown. Ageism is detrimental to all of us, but particularly to the queer community because we are not necessarily given the opportunity to appreciate our bodies as young people. Queer spaces are often very youth-oriented and it's important to recognize that our bodies don't suddenly lose all value past our thirties.

Youth is lovely in its own way, but for many of us (myself included) our lives don't fully feel like our own until we are older. Getting older is such an invigorating thought to me, and a changing body is just part of that. We deserve to love our bodies at any age; there is no expiry date on accepting yourself.

For me, the answer to the question 'Has accepting your sexuality allowed you to become more accepting of your body?' is a thousand times 'Yes'. Coming out opened the door for me to start focusing on how I felt about myself beyond the male gaze and find communities that accepted me. However, we all have different experiences with our sexuality and body image and this isn't the case for everyone.

Here are the responses to the same question from the people I interviewed.

When I came out to my peers I was 15 years old. It negatively impacted my body image as I felt I didn't fit into the norms I would see on Tumblr or in gay porn. I felt like an outsider to my straight peers and like an outsider to the queer world. I didn't feel like a chubby ginger girl had any real place in finding or deserving love.

Annie Wade-Smith (she/they)

Yes! My body is for me and me alone. I was always trying to fit my body for the expectations of the general society. As I grew and discovered myself and my sexuality, especially my demisexuality, I learnt that it's another step in my free, individual expression.

Kelsey Ellison (she/her)

Other than the external influences and my advocacy work, my relationship between my body and my sexuality are quite separate. I never really had any hang-ups about being gay, but had thousands about being fat. If anything, the more ingrained in gay/queer culture I have become over the years, the more I've been aware of body image disparity as a wider issue, and it's made me want to change the way we view it. It feels wider than my personal body image.

James Makings (he/him)

Over years, yes. When I first came out, I was made more insecure about my body. I felt like I finally got to grips with beating diet culture's beauty ideals in the straight world, but once I came out it was an entirely new beast to face.

Gay men are often pushed into certain stereotypes, from 'skinny twink' to 'masc 4 masc', with little in-between. It was incredibly hard for me to find belonging even within my own community and I was left feeling like both my body and femininity were the issue. Over time I have grown to express and love all sides of myself. I feel that LGBTQIA+ folk are used to a level of adversity sadly, so when they get to a place where they express themselves 100 per cent authentically they're proud of that and willing to defend it daily. Our existence isn't up for discussion.

Stevie Blaine (he/him)

My sexuality has helped me understand my presentation a lot more and explore new fashion styles, patterns, and so on. I think accepting I was a lesbian helped me find myself, which may be obvious to many, but to myself I harboured a lot of hate about being a lesbian. Once that hate turned into acceptance, I started to explore my presentation to the world. In terms of my body, I'm very fortunate to be in a long-term relationship and she loves my body, but without her, I wouldn't be as loving towards it.

Charl Summers (she/her)

I've never had much of a problem with my asexuality, so I don't think there was a point where I accepted it and anything in particular changed. I think my appearance has always been politicized as a Black woman; and as an alternative Black woman, it's always been something that makes a statement and gets a mixed reception. I've always said that my asexuality was never the weirdest thing about me for that reason. It was a layer in my self-acceptance, but not the top layer, I had a lot of other things influencing the way I had to navigate society and a lot of other things that influenced people's perceptions.

Yasmin Benoit (she/her)

In some ways, I think my sexuality – or more specifically, having partners that are not cisgender men – has helped me accept my body more. The reason why is this: when I feel insecure about something with my body, I ask myself if I would have found that thing unattractive in someone else, and the answer is always no. In terms of my presentation, I do not feel I present differently, but I understand that, for some, coming out also means they 'find themselves' more in terms of how they feel comfortable presenting, and that is beautiful.

Amalie Lee (she/her)

Accepting my sexuality as a bisexual woman was very liberating. Suddenly, being 'different' and standing out was desirable on some level because it was almost validating. I didn't want to be seen as someone straight – that felt 'normal' and I didn't want that. In hindsight, I think standing out was less scary because then I didn't have to come out and point out that somebody had made the wrong assumption.

Mia Violet (she/her)

We are led to believe that our sexuality is somehow disconnected from our identity, particularly if we are queer. Whilst
heterosexuality is freely talked about and considered innate,
the connection that queer people have with their sexuality is
considered too loud, too brash, too forced. I think that is a big
reason why it took me years even after coming out to really see
how I felt about my body as at all linked to my sexual orientation. The freedom that came with accepting who I was also
steered me down a path of accepting my body for what it was.
Engaging with queer communities was also one of the most
valuable things I could do for my body image because I began
to realize that the thin, white, cis women I had seen represented
in the media are only a small part of who we are. Seeing diverse
queer bodies and seeing the power in them was life-changing.

Gender Roles?
In This Economy?

Okay, so... Not to digress into my first-year English student self, but I have a Judith Butler quote for you. Butler was bound to come up sooner or later because their work was probably the first critical feminist theory I encountered that made me question my own queerness. Frankly, at 19 years old I barely understood half of it, nodding along because I was too afraid to say I didn't know what was going on. So, I tried really hard to at least sound like I understood. I knew I was queer at that point but I was still absolutely and vociferously denying it.

The lady doth protest too much.

I was struggling with certain parts of feminist theory at that age and I think some of the older texts didn't really gel with my own concept of what it was to be a woman. In fact, the kinds of strict boundaries of what it meant to be a woman informed my own rejections of certain gender notions and allowed me to begin processing myself outside of the gender norms expected of me.

I decided to read *Undoing Gender* by Judith Butler and I came across a quote that stuck with me for years afterwards:

Let's face it. We're undone by each other. And if we're not, we're missing something... One does not always stay intact. It may be that one wants to, or does, but it may also be that despite one's best efforts, one is undone, in the face of the other. (Butler 2004, p.19)

It made me confront the idea of grief, and grieving the loss of the person you thought you were so you can accept the person you really are. Grief, in my opinion, is a useful framework for being able to describe those great changes you go through within yourself in which you know you are doing the right thing but are simultaneously saying goodbye to a life you might have once expected for yourself. Some examples of this for me:

- *Recovering from an eating disorder:* I was holding onto the image of a person who wasn't real, in the desperate hope I would become them. I had to grieve the loss of someone I was never going to be. It was a good thing, but I had to change my outlook on myself and on my own body.

- *Being openly queer:* I realized that I felt like I was often per-forming heterosexuality. I was unable to be particularly open about my queerness and eventually that was just too much for me. However, there were people in my past I had to let go of in the process of coming out. There was a life that was once safe which suddenly wasn't. It was all in the name of coming to terms with myself, but it was no less painful. Sometimes it hurts to do the right thing.

- *Realizing that whatever kind of womanhood I was told I had to conform to, I absolutely didn't:* Just because my body was consistently coded as feminine, it didn't mean that my gender identity reflected that. There was a lot of fear around realizing just how fluid I was and I had to grieve an image of myself I had attempted to curate over the years.

When Butler talks about being undone by each other, 19-year-old me probably didn't understand the fullness of meaning there; but what I knew was that relationships with others – especially other queer people – was something that I needed to come to terms with for myself and my body.

Other queer people help us come to terms with ourselves. Fat queer women who I am close to helped me re-imagine queer bodies through our late-night conversations about our identities over wine and pizza, and meeting my partner meant I put work into understanding trans and non-binary identity more deeply, subsequently realizing that I myself needed to address my feelings about gender. Masculine-presenting women in my life – without even realizing it – made me feel more confident in exploring my presentation.

Queer Body Positivity has always transcended traditional gender roles, whether that be through the art of drag, through the grassroots work of trans and non-binary people, or through queer relationships that simply cannot align with heteropatriarchal standards. The binary idea of what men's bodies are, what women's bodies are, and how they interact, is often thrown out of the window when it comes to queerness.

Gender and queer liberation will always be intertwined, as will gender and the body. If we want to focus on body liberation as queer people, then really it is trans and non-binary people paving the way. To resist something as utterly stifling and structural as a heteropatriarchal model of gender is to resist many of the boundaries that society places on our bodies. This is not to say that if you are trans, you find yourself suddenly exempt from these boundaries – in fact, I have many stories in this book about the increased pressure trans people are under to conform. However, liberation from the idea that gender is something ascribed to your body without your consent is groundbreaking.

How do gender norms affect how the LGBTQ+ community feel about their bodies?

Sometimes I wonder if, in a different time, I would have identified differently or would have been unable to show my true self to the world at all. I think about all those queer people who are recorded on census or in their obituaries as people that they weren't. When we look at statistics now, more and more people are openly shunning traditional ideas of gendered bodies, in a way that our queer ancestors couldn't.

Anybody saying that trans and non-binary people just popped into existence in the last ten years clearly doesn't read any good literature.

Gender is very strangely sacred in our society. The binary genders and their relationship to genitalia are apparently natural yet need to be strictly enforced lest they break down. So, of course, these rigid boundaries are made of glass and queer people – who love collecting small, interesting items – have just the right rocks to throw at them. Gender norms have significant effects on how we perceive ourselves and our bodies and, from a personal perspective, I find nothing more enjoyable than completely ignoring them.

As I will outline further in my chapter discussing eating disorders, 'Our Complex Relationship with Food', the LGBTQ+ community are deeply affected by the way in which our bodies are coded, both within our own communities and among cishet people. Some of the issues that affect LGBTQ+ people in terms of gender and our bodies are:

- the pressures among queer men to conform to a certain type of masculinity

- the pressures among queer women to conform to a certain type of femininity, alongside internalized misogyny

- the idea that non-binary people owe the world androgyny and fit into a 'third gender' category

- the expectation that trans people must present as cisgender in order to be respected

- the expectation that trans people must have gender reassignment surgery in order to be valid

- difficulties receiving healthcare, based on gender

- issues of safety in public if queer bodies do not conform to a heteronormative standard.

Gender roles affect all queer people and I have felt unsettled by the increasing burden of what 'womanhood' supposedly meant as I became an adult. The more my body changed, the more expectations of some idealized femininity felt like a great current trying to drag me down. However, before I get into how gender has affected my own feelings about my body, I want to go a little bit into gender dysphoria and body dysmorphia for queer people, as it is a very important topic.

Sometimes, dysphoria and dysmorphia can be confused with one another and they can also overlap.

Gender dysphoria refers to heightened unease and dissatisfaction in your gender. This can be a huge contributing factor to mental health issues in trans people but it is more complex than simply a dissatisfaction with your body. Even though gender dysphoria can be very intertwined with body dissatisfaction, it is not synonymous with body dysmorphia.

Body dysmorphia refers to a mental health issue that causes you to perceive your body as flawed, and it really distorts the way you see yourself. Body dysmorphic disorder often makes you think that your body looks a certain way, even with evidence to the contrary. Because of this, body dysmorphia is very prevalent among people who have eating disorders. It is a specific mental health condition.

These issues can and do coincide with one another, particularly in terms of feeling dysphoric over certain physical traits that are gendered, even when others don't see your body as such. Living with a trans person who has experienced different levels of dysphoria throughout our relationship has really helped me understand how they feel about their body and how gender-coded body traits can really heighten that feeling.

Another useful thing to talk about is *gender euphoria* – the opposite of dysphoria – which refers to the positive feeling around someone's true gender identity. Again, this can be strongly linked to body image and presentation.

I asked Mia Violet about her first experiences with gender euphoria.

The first moment of body euphoria was on a trip to London for a convention. I had brought loud and dramatic clothes with me in case I felt brave enough to wear them. But I didn't. I spent the first day wearing bland clothes that weren't much different than my usual ones. On the second day I knew I would be annoyed at myself later if I went home without at least trying to wear the fun gothic clothes I'd brought. That helped me push through the fear and wear them out of my hotel room. As soon as I saw my reflection, I was hit with so much joy and giddy energy, I thought it must be the happiest I'd ever felt.

Mia Violet (she/her)

It isn't always easy to know exactly how you are feeling about your body when you are feeling it and, from a queer perspective, we can harbour a lot of repressed feelings about gender and our bodies that need unpacking. This chapter will open up the floor to some trans people who have had different experiences with their personal feelings about their bodies, healthcare, recovery and the barriers that trans bodies are met with in our society. One of my favourite parts about talking with people about this subject is learning about the different ways queer people truly come to terms with bodies that don't fit cisheteronormative standards. Personal body acceptance is possible regardless of your gender, and even though we all have different hurdles, it is important to make that statement.

Yes, you can feel positive about your body and your gender identity in ways that maybe you wouldn't have expected. This is coming from someone who couldn't imagine feeling comfortable in the fluidity of their gender and presentation even a few years ago.

Gender and healthcare

Healthcare is something that isn't always brought up in mainstream Body Positivity conversations, but it's such a vital issue. As a person who is chronically ill and queer, this is something that is at the forefront of my own experiences. As well as dealing with gender-related healthcare, trans people can often end up struggling with general medical issues.

I decided to speak with trans activists, models and creatives about their varying experiences.

> I was incredibly lucky to go private for my entire medical transition throughout my teens. It meant that when I was 16 I had 21 exams for my GCSEs, and two days after my final exam I flew overseas to have my gender affirming surgery at the best practice in the world. That was an intense time, and made passing my ten-year anniversary in June all the sweeter. I look at how far I've come, and how validated I feel because of the privileges afforded to me with having this healthcare during my teens. It was absolutely the right thing for me and has meant a life of relative normality in my adulthood.
>
> *Maxine Heron (she/her)*

> My title (Mx) and pronouns (they/them) often get overlooked or dismissed. As a trans and/or non-binary person, you have to constantly go through the traumatic experience of explaining yourself over and over again. It is exhausting, triggering and damaging. When you do get that odd person using your correct title and/or pronouns, it almost seems like the best thing ever. However, this should be a norm and it shouldn't be that people like myself get this feeling once in a while. Either people get denied certain healthcare and etiquettes that everyone should receive regardless of how they identify, or other experiences get dismissed onto your gender/identity. As a trans person you have to go through 'hell' to try and obtain procedures and/or help towards being more yourself (for example, relevant gender affirmation surgeries), whereas a cisgender person does not have to go through this or have

their mental health questioned to obtain a body that would make them happier (for example, cosmetic surgeries).

TJ Lucas-Box (they/them)

Being trans in the healthcare system has turned me into a liar. I am used to walking into a room and knowing more than the healthcare professional about what I need, and that includes knowing what they want and don't want to hear. I lie and perform to get the care that I need, which is a depressing testament to how poor trans healthcare is.

Mia Violet (she/her)

I mean there's the struggle to get gender affirming healthcare, about which much has been written... The three- to four-year wait times... The cost of going private... Malpractice, abuse and complete lack of understanding from cis doctors deciding whether you're trans enough, etc., etc. But then there's non-transition-related care too. The system just isn't set up for us. For example, as a trans man I've experienced the following:

- I've been forced to open a completely new medical record in order to have a 'Mr' title. So that now when I ring up about a medical issue I've had for years, it's not on my record, and I have to disclose my deadname and get them to reopen my old record. I also got a letter assuming I'd just arrived in the country, due to the newness of my record, which instructed me I needed to pay for my healthcare as a non-UK citizen. This was obviously xenophobic (thanks, Theresa May) as well as being another issue of trans healthcare.

- I've had to fight really hard to get an intravaginal scan

at the hospital. My GP's system wouldn't allow them to book me for one because my gender marker was 'M', and 'men don't have vaginas' according to the booking system. So, my GP kept booking me for pelvic scans, writing that I was a trans man in the notes...which the hospital then wouldn't read, and would repeatedly book me for the wrong scan. In the end, I had to plead with someone at the hospital to book the correct scan for me – again, disclosing to another stranger my status and talking about my junk with them! It's a nightmare.

Jackson King (he/him)

Gender and healthcare has many different layers, as Jackson puts so well. For trans people, it is not just gender affirming healthcare that is difficult, but *all* healthcare. The systems that are in place are just not built for trans people, but it need not be that way. There is a lot of stress around going to the doctor for trans people and, as someone who lives with a trans person, I have often had to check if the GP is trans-friendly and if certain tests will be dealt with sensitively. From the perspective of privacy and bodily autonomy, it can become really difficult to keep your boundaries in place but it is important that you know you deserve them. It is okay to be upset, frustrated, uncomfortable, and even to dissociate from your body in healthcare situations that are triggering or traumatic. We have to be kind to ourselves in situations like this, because sometimes there is nothing else we can do.

One of the issues I have often faced with healthcare is the disclosure of my queerness and the worry that brings. This usually happens with any healthcare situation in which I'm asked about my sexual activity or if I might be pregnant. Healthcare professionals will usually not take a simple 'no' for an answer and I must eventually, rather awkwardly, explain why it is impossible for me to be pregnant. It might seem like an insignificant point, but the fear of having healthcare professionals who are not accepting is very real when these people have control over how your body is cared for.

Having other people to fight your corner when dealing with healthcare as a queer person is so helpful. It can be hard for us to fight for ourselves when we feel vulnerable, but as someone who has a chronic illness, I value the people who have helped me find my strength in tough situations with my body.

Gender-inclusive healthcare will save lives in many different ways.

How has my experience with gender affected my body image?

So, there was this dress. I can see it swimming in front of my eyes, I can remember the cotton fabric, the cheap seams unravelling. It was some fast-fashion dress I bought when I was 15 years old, I think. I must have been young when I bought it, because I had stretched it out over the years, even wearing it well into my days at university.

The dress was navy-blue with huge white flowers dotted about it. It cinched in my waist and swam around the top of my thighs, always making me slightly anxious that it would blow up like Marilyn Monroe's dress. Except not in a cute or fun way.

Every time I wore this dress, all the people I came across complimented me about it. It was everyone's favourite dress on me and people would always fawn over how it suited my shape. Boyfriends liked it more than any other dress on me, and whenever I put it on I would always get that little nod of appreciation for my body.

The thing is, I fucking hated that dress.

When I think about wearing that bloody dress, it makes my skin crawl. I always remember that dress as a mask. It absolutely wasn't me, and my driving force for wearing it was that other people reinforced the idea that it was what I should wear. There was nothing malicious in it – how could they have known how I felt if I didn't even really know myself? I felt so uncomfortable in my body when I wore that dress but I absolutely could not place why. Now, it all makes a lot more sense to me: I was performing as something I wasn't and I was coded by others in a way that made my whole body hot and itchy like I just wanted to wriggle out of their perception entirely.

I realized that my version of what it meant to be a girl really didn't fit what that meant to others. Some days, I woke up, saw my feminine wardrobe and thought, 'Great, this works perfectly,' and other days I had nothing to wear because it wasn't me. I channelled all that unease into my body. On those days when I felt like womanhood was a costume, I told myself that it was because I wasn't thin enough, my hips were too big, my boobs were too obvious. I thought I needed to change my body rather than address what was really obvious looking back.

I'm fluid as hell. I'm naturally fluid in every damn way, gender and sexuality. I really didn't know that you are allowed to be so changeable, and my focus on being at a fixed point forever was so detrimental to me. Giving myself permission to be who I really am, and truly know myself, changed how I saw my body. Learning that my gender isn't defined by how other people see me was freeing. I spent far too long thinking that because I had boobs I couldn't openly access my masculinity without being called a fraud. I also felt that I had to perform femininity after being told my only worth in this world was based around how sexually appealing cishet men found me.

If I am being honest, I knew how fluid I was when I was a little kid. And I knew when I was being told that baggy t-shirts and jeans 'didn't suit my figure' that people considered me more worthy and beautiful when I was embracing femininity. These ideas were consistently reinforced by people throughout my life and I began to feel like the only way people would like me was if I presented within the parameters of a cishet woman.

Something I remember very clearly is feeling uncomfortable with womanhood being so focused on the reproductive purpose of my body. I never wanted to give birth to children, but I was always told I should be extremely pleased that I had childbearing hips. I was lucky, apparently, because that was what mattered. So, I tried to come to terms with the idea that I wanted to give birth, when really I didn't. My body was being taken away from me and I began to hide this little voice inside me that was saying:

'This is not who you are.'

'This is not what you want.'

'You are not this girl that they think you are.'

As I got older and began dating boys, I felt like I had to perform femininity even further to be loved and accepted. Queerness itself wasn't even on my radar at that time, I had poured all my energy into slimming myself down and anxiously buying clothes that I thought boys might find sexy. The hilarious thing about this, as well as being a bit sad, is that I didn't even find boys sexy! It really wasn't until I was in my mid-twenties that I began to realize just how little I ever focused on how I felt about my own gender and presentation.

We are unwittingly born into a heteronormative narrative. It is often the narrative of our parents, our friends, our society. It takes a long time to unpick that and it is okay if you don't figure that out straight away. It took me years to realize how much my obsession with thinness was centred around controlling how others saw me.

I knew I was being seen as a hyperfeminine woman who would bear children. And I knew that wasn't me.

Truthfully, there will be people in this world who will want to define your gender by what you look like. They will probably kick and scream about it too. However, as with everything, they don't get to define you. Honestly, should we really be letting the way other people interpret the fleshy vessel that transports us through the world define our whole freaking identity? That's absurd!

Are those people you? No. So it has nothing to do with them. Your body doesn't exist just to prove something to someone else.

Stories about gender and body image

Where would this chapter be without some words from other queer people about how their gender and body image are intertwined?

> There's a huge amount of trans men who don't give a fuck and aren't afraid to enjoy femme things. It can be complicated with gender dysphoria, because sometimes wearing a certain femme item might trigger it, so you can't do it – which is a different thing to conforming to hegemonic masculinity. I think queer trans men in particular tend to be more free and playful with gender expression – just like many cisgender queer men are. Whereas I think straight trans men can struggle with this. Just like cisgender straight men.
>
> *Jackson King (he/him)*

I'd say [trans women] are even more susceptible to patriarchal beauty standards than cis women are. We have so much more to prove with our womanhood. And seeing what the pinnacle of female or femininity is, and where this affirmation in our gender can supposedly be found, is entirely enforced in the cishet mainstream media. It's why we must continue to uphold trans women as also setting their own kind of beauty standards, and continue to incorporate trans women in mainstream media to prove to the rest of the world that we and our beauty are valid, too.

Maxine Heron (she/her)

The stereotypical look of a lesbian is that of a butch lesbian, and as someone who very much enjoys 'feminine' clothing, I could not be further from fitting this mould. I think there can be this belief that if you're a lesbian you should always be outwardly showing this by how you dress, whether that be in a 'masculine' way or covering yourself in rainbows. While I am proud of my sexuality and will never hide it, I will also always be true to myself by wearing what makes me feel comfortable in my own skin.

Molly Elizabeth Agnew (she/her)

There is massive pressure inside and outside of the trans community to conform and reject traditional femininity in different ways. In the community I've been questioned and teased for enjoying stereotypical 'girly' aesthetics and fashion. People have seen it as strange, and expected that at this later stage in my transition I should have settled on wearing simple androgynous clothes. Essentially, my femininity is looked at as a potential overcompensation and 'unnecessary', and not as the valid and genuine expression of myself that it is. In cis circles, my love of girly stuff is mostly overlooked – people usually see it as normal or endearing. But occasionally, someone who doesn't know me can see my presentation as my attempt to make up for lost time or as something I'm doing ignorantly.

Mia Violet (she/her)

At the start of my baby gay experiences, I felt so much pressure as a femme queer woman to present myself as queer. On some of my first nights out in queer spaces, I was ridiculed by other queer women as I didn't look gay; I have been turned away from gay bars because I look straight – I felt my appearance was gatekeeping me from all these amazing experiences I heard about online. But now I hold more confidence in my presentation to the world. If someone judges me based on my appearance, that's their ignorance showing and I don't have to burden myself with that.

Charl Summers (she/her)

Becoming accepting of my sexuality has allowed me to become more open with my body and the exploration of my body. I've grown to explore my femininity, whether it be in clothing, imagery, body expression, makeup, etc. In turn this has helped me to deconstruct the toxic masculine lessons and contrasts I have learned from society and sport, and rebuild a healthy masculinity that I can love and appreciate. I can love my masculinity without it feeling like a prison, a list of things I can't do and can't be. I can explore and love my femininity, knowing it makes me no less man and no less me.

R.K. Russell (he/him)

I think a majority of society currently assumes 'non-binary' identities are those who only appear aesthetically 'fluid' and/or 'ambiguous' in their gender expression. This is wrong. Non-binary humans can express in many different forms/ways, whether that be 'femme', 'masc', both and/or neither. I am 'transmasc, non-binary'. This means I don't associate with the 'sex' I was assigned with at birth (AFAB). However, I also don't identify as a 'binary male'. I also identify with the 'non-binary' term because of this, but also because I still currently feel that I also have a more 'fluid' aesthetic. I think there is an overall pressure to conform to one thing and there are also 'gatekeepers', even within the 'trans world' too. This can be very difficult for people who identify as anything in-between the binaries. There are also wrong expectations of people and hormones. It should be seen that whether someone decides to take hormones or not, it does not change their identity as a trans and/or non-binary person.

TJ Lucas-Box (they/them)

Your gender suits you

There is a lot to unpack when it comes to gender and our bodies. That is probably the most obvious statement ever, but what can I say... I'm a social media person. I love a good bitesize thought that can fit into a Twitter post. In our current climate, talking openly about the intricacies of gender is...difficult. We are being set back by people who have not taken the time to critically think about these topics and unfortunately are often unwilling to listen. This may be making it harder for some of you reading this book to feel comfortable and safe coming out or to be able to work through your feelings about your body.

I get that.

People who are prescriptive and oppressive about gender boundaries negatively affect us all. When it comes to self-reflecting on how your gender and body image are entwined, it is often a reflection on all those times you distorted yourself to appease the wants and desires of those around you. You have to untangle yourself from all those knots you twisted yourself into in order to attempt to exist easily in the world.

But it was never easy. It was a false ease, an invented ease. There is nothing easy about hiding your authentic self. At the very least, you deserve autonomy over your body and your gender. That's literally the bare minimum. You deserve the space to fucking understand yourself, to receive competent, empathetic healthcare and to actually...you know...explore who you are. This is where the LGBTQ+ community needs to stick together to uplift and protect every queer body.

Don't forget you are amazing and your gender suits you.

Our Complex Relationship with Food

Could I really have written a book about body image without mentioning food?

Food...

Food is not only integral to our lives because it keeps us alive, but it is also where our culture and comfort are carried with us. As a Greek-English person, I think of sweet melomakarona at Christmas, tsoureki at Easter, but also a jam buttie and a cup of tea after school. One bite of comfort food can take you back to moments you might have forgotten or to the memories of people who are long gone. And yet, food is also so heavy in our society, holding the weight of expectation, sadness and fear.

There is so much to be unpacked.

There is a difference between disordered eating and actually having an eating disorder. However, disordered eating behaviours can be a precursor to an eating disorder (Zucker 2018). This issue is very nuanced and definitely requires trained people to make any diagnosis, but it is good to mention that someone might have disordered eating behaviours rather than an eating disorder. The lines can most definitely be blurred, but there are some disordered behaviours which are normalized by our society and can lead to a more serious eating disorder:

- feeling shame and guilt eating certain foods
- consistently dieting or yo-yo dieting
- restrictive diets and elimination diets (e.g. completely eliminating certain food groups)
- consistent concerns over weight and body image
- food restriction for the purposes of weight loss.

These behaviours might sound completely normal, considering our society is so hell-bent on us restricting our food intake, but they really aren't. 'Normal' eating behaviours tend to mean that you don't place morality onto food and, rather than putting things into food boxes of 'good' and 'bad', all food is seen as more neutral. People without disordered eating behaviours are in tune with their body's hunger and therefore eat intuitively (Zucker 2018). There are some great studies and resources on this subject but this section is just to give an overview of the differences when I talk about disordered eating behaviours and then full-blown eating disorders, such as anorexia nervosa.

According to NEDA (2021), we as LGBTQ+ people, particularly during the teenage years, have a higher risk of eating disorders than our cishet counterparts. There is yet to be a wealth of research, of course, as is the way with many LGBTQ+ issues, but what is there so far shows that we are suffering and we are suffering without many resources. Our experiences with violence, trauma and discrimination are shown to greatly elevate our vulnerability to eating disorders, alongside pressures from within our community. There is also the added issue of high body dissatisfaction. As I wrote in the previous chapter, stressors that come with being a queer person – fear of coming out, internalized homophobia and transphobia, rejection, harassment, bullying – all contribute to our mental health and body image.

Eating disorders are some of the most common and most detrimental mental illnesses. In fact, anorexia nervosa has the highest mortality rate of any mental illness (Anorexia Bulimia Care n.d.). Eating disorders are also mostly likely to form during adolescence – a time that can be so devastating for the mental health of young queer people. My queer friends and I often talk about experiencing our teens in our twenties because we were unable to experience our teenage years as our true selves. This reminds me of just how much young LGBTQ+ people can suffer during some of the most pivotal moments in their development.

Don't get me wrong... I think that many young people today have a very different experience of adolescence than people of my generation did. The spectre of Section 28 is not quite so haunting. (Section 28 was a British law implemented by Margaret Thatcher, which was in place between 1988 and 2003. It prohibited 'promoting homosexuality' in schools by teaching or by publishing material and it meant that it was illegal to even talk about homosexuality in schools.)

I am a young millennial but alas, there are no more teenage millennials. I was not out as a teenager and I would have been far too afraid to contemplate it. I look back and wonder how much of my own body dissatisfaction came not from being queer but from trying so hard not to be.

But you don't look sick

Eating disorders are not just the illness of thin, white, cishet young women. However, they are seemingly the only people given space in recovery. Images of young girls with anorexia as the posters for all eating disorders can be damaging when a variety of complex mental illnesses are reduced to looking a specific way. I say this as someone who, when they were very ill, strove to be that emaciated young girl who was both pitied and admired. Admiration from society for what is perceived to be self-control is really an admiration for thinness. Eating disorders, however, are not thinness, they are not whiteness, they are not heterosexuality, they are not gendered. Relationships with food are complex, and such a personal relationship cannot simply be read on someone's body.

An impactful moment for me as a queer person was when I watched the drag queens on *RuPaul's Drag Race* have an honest and frank conversation about eating disorders. The way in which a fresh sense of camaraderie and understanding was cultivated through opening up about this issue reminded me of my first moments online, when it felt like a breath of fresh air to finally admit that I was suffering. Shea Coulee's words in Season 9, Episode 5 (2017) have stuck with me since that moment:

> I was feeling all these pressures [from] the beauty standards that exist within the gay community, and it's something I had a lot of shame about...sometimes, people don't understand that, though we come across as these really strong, beautiful creatures, sometimes we're really struggling on the inside.

I cannot help but feel a deep sense of sadness and pain every time another person admits that they have been struggling with food. When I began my work online in eating disorder recovery, I did not expect so many strangers to suddenly feel so comfortable admitting how hard it was for them to cope. It felt like I had created a space with my own honesty that allowed others to be honest too, and in a way, they helped me as much as I helped them. I spent so long believing I would never recover and always feel that sense of shame in my stomach. However, one vital thing to remember is:

You can recover. You do not have to suffer for your entire life. There is work that can be done. There is no such thing as a lost cause.

Maybe it's a wellness choice, maybe it's a diet

Now, you may not struggle with eating – many people do not and yet have an unhealthy relationship with food. However, our society has this knack for packaging disordered eating with a nice little bow and marketing it as a healthy diet. Sometimes it will be advertised as a healthy eating plan. Sometimes it will be some wild new ploy by a celebrity which means you have to cut out any foods with a red hue (or something). What I am saying in this case is that disordered eating is not only normalized but *worshipped* in our society, so that makes recognizing it all the more difficult. Recognizing that you are struggling and you don't need to be is a huge task and one that took me years.

The point of me writing this is to give space to some self-reflection, just for a moment. Particularly in terms of mental health, it is very easy to convince yourself you're fine when maybe you are not. I do it all the time. Sometimes I wake up feeling like the whole world is against me, burst into tears, get back into bed, then try to tell myself it's not depression. It's that part of the film where the narrator says, 'She thinks she doesn't have depression, but she really does. Let's see how long it takes her to figure it out.' It can be hard to admit that you are dealing with disordered eating, even to yourself, because the world constantly normalizes disordered behaviours. As Shea Couleé said, there is a lot of shame around eating disorders and disordered eating, and it is sometimes easier to just convince yourself you are disciplined or you *need* the sense of control it brings you so you can function.

My advice is not a resource from a doctor who can diagnose you. This is just a perspective from someone who has suffered and often tried to convince themselves they were okay when they were not. It is always useful to take a beat and engage with what you are feeling if you are struggling.

There are lots of reasons why we suffer and it is not just about weight loss

For me, weight loss had a lot to do with falling into an eating disorder, but it certainly was not the only factor. As I grew up, I started reflecting on my feelings about my body and my relationship with food.

Here are some of my own realizations:

- I felt very out of control of my own identity and my own life. I was being bullied at school because of my weight, I felt that my identity didn't gel with the person I was on the outside and I felt a kind of toxic comfort in fixating on food.

- Puberty was changing my body in a way I found uncomfortable, and the fact that I developed breasts and wider hips when I was young meant I was also sexualized very early on. I thought that by making my body smaller, I would be taking my body back from those who sexualized me against my will.

- I was afraid of eating in front of people after being called a 'pig' because I was chubby.

- Recurring traumatic periods of my life saw me return to disordered eating patterns again and again. I often saw restrictive eating as self-soothing during those times.

- I wanted to have a smaller body in order to present in a more masculine way. At that time in my life I thought you had to be thin to be masculine-presenting.

For queer people, there are often added layers to our experiences with food and weight loss. There is medical stigma that can stop us from seeking treatment – an issue that is particularly prevalent in trans communities – and a lack of representation and LGBTQ+ specific research, which means the signs are more likely to be ignored.

Take this as a sign that you absolutely do not deserve to be ignored. Even if you are struggling a little bit, even if you feel like you are mostly fine, you still deserve to be granted the space to heal.

How do eating disorders/diet culture affect the LGBTQ+ community?

Let's get into the facts and stats before I continue. Well, let's talk about the facts and stats that we actually have and go on from there.

The PRIDE Study (2017–) is an ongoing, comprehensive study

on LGBTQ+ mental and physical health and their work is really useful for understanding the broader issues that affect LGBTQ+ people. The LGBTQ+ community is not treated as a monolith in this study and it allows us to look at how different parts of the community function. However, we are still at a point in time where studies into LGBTQ+ mental health are limited. A lot of these studies are still quite binary – often focusing on just men and women – but this is indicative of a lack of research in queer mental health on a bigger scale. There is also, unsurprisingly, more research on cisgender people than on trans people. I'm going to go through some of the studies I think are relevant to understanding how eating disorders affect our communities, and that will be a good way to move into my own experiences and stories from other queer people.

Studies in cisgender gay men

In 2019, there was a study in the eating disorder attitudes and behaviours among gay men. This study was specifically for cisgender gay men and did not include cisgender bisexual or transgender men. It showed that 20 per cent of those in the study engaged in dietary restraint, 11 per cent in binge eating and 10 per cent in excessive exercise (Nagata *et al.* 2019). Studies suggest that compared with heterosexual men, queer men are pressured to conform to a more traditionally athletic, muscular body type and that this emphasis negatively affects their body image. Furthermore, queer men are more likely to exhibit eating disorder symptoms than heterosexual men, due to fatphobia within the community and the pressure to maintain a thin body. As with most groups in the LGBTQ+ community, higher rates of anxiety and depression are often inextricably linked to body obsession and disordered eating.

I spoke with James Makings about what conversations he feels we need to be having around gay men's body image.

> All marketing to gay men features the same body types, and TV and films only show a certain body type in gay men. This, combined with the fact that, in gay male culture, sex is very prominent, leads to a seriously unhealthy relationship with body image that tells us that fat is wrong and we should all strive to have perfectly gym-honed bodies. And, frankly, even those guys with 'perfect bodies' are riddled with body issues and eating disorders too. That, I guess, is the double-edged sword of being the more prominent group in the LGBTQ+ community. It seems that lesbians, for example, have been able to cultivate their own rules around image that seem a lot more free and positive; and, of course, the cornerstone in being queer/non-binary is being yourself fully, so that also seems unbridled by community-specific ideals about body image. So, in terms of conversations within the LGBTQ+ community, I think we need to give fat gay men a seat at the table again, because it seems we've been largely forgotten.
>
> James Makings (he/him)

I'm going to address this more in the next chapter, which specifically addresses fatphobia, but anti-fatness is such an important part of why people struggle with their eating. As a queer femme, I definitely feel that there is a strong, positive culture around body image from other queer women and femmes; and, in general, Body Positive communities are mostly made up of women. When it comes to genuine Body Positive messages, very few focus on men, which means the conversations are not necessarily going further within those communities.

Studies in transgender men and women

In a vast survey of 300,000 college students in the USA, it was found that transgender students reported much higher rates of eating disorder diagnoses and behaviours than their cisgender counterparts (McCallum Place 2020). It is widely recognized that trans people suffer exponentially with disordered eating, yet the support for trans mental health issues is limited. In 2020, a study in the eating attitudes of transgender men and women showed that, in the 28 days before the study, 25 per cent of trans men were dieting and 28 per cent of trans women were dieting (Nagata *et al.* 2020b). This study was specifically in binary trans people. There are separate studies that focus on gender non-conforming folks, though it is not a widely researched area. In terms of behaviours, trans men were reported to be more prone to binge eating than the general population, whereas trans women were reported as engaging with dieting and excessive exercise. Although not all trans people wish to change their bodies, body dysphoria is a huge component of body dissatisfaction in this community. Understandably, this is one of the reasons why trans people have higher rates of eating disorders (this was unpacked further in the previous chapter, 'Gender Roles? In This Economy?'). A lot of studies also suggest that experiences of minority stress, trauma, discrimination and violence are all really key factors when discussing eating disorders in the trans community. Eating disorders are very complex and it is too simplistic to assume that they are entirely based around weight and nothing else – there are often deeper issues at play.

I spoke with model Maxine Heron about how she has struggled with food throughout her life.

> For me it was always about control. It was a secret that I was able to go until 5 p.m. without eating a thing – like it was a challenge I was practising for and regularly winning at. I didn't realize what an unshakeable vice starving myself is, and I didn't know it'd continue to follow me for the next decade. I still feel a pang of relief when my stomach grumbles – a bizarre 'Oh, still got it!' mentality. It was less about meeting beauty standards, and more about feeling as though I refused to give in. I can always tell when I'm having a truly happy period in my life, because when the hunger comes, I eat without hesitation. I still grapple with calorie counting and feeling as though I've failed some days, but my progression with my body has come such a long way since school when hating food and hating myself was all that I really knew.
>
> *Maxine Heron (she/her)*

I also spoke with Mia Violet about her relationship between her body image and eating disorder growing up.

> I made a link between my eating habits and the look of my body on a positive to negative scale. Or at least that's what I thought. I actually had no positive thoughts, but endless negative ones where I'd blame any 'flaws' in my complexion, body shape, or function as a result of my inability to resist eating 'bad food'. There was a time in my late teens when I was confused about how I actually looked. Family would call me 'bean pole' as an intended endearing tease, or they'd joke at mealtimes that I needed to eat more as I was so thin. But I felt overweight. I didn't see myself as thin. I considered myself

somebody who ate a lot and had the body as a direct result. It made me feel that my body must be deformed, that maybe I had skinny limbs but then under my clothes I was huge.

Mia Violet (she/her)

Studies in gender expansive/non-binary people

A study in December 2020 looked into the way gender expansive people (anyone who does not identify with the binary genders) engage with food and body image. This study is interesting as it focuses on restrictive eating as well as concern about body shape. Body shape in our society is so intrinsically linked to gender – people often code you very quickly from the shape of your body, so it is no surprise that this is a particularly important issue for non-binary people. The study also shows that nearly one in four gender expansive people ate less food to influence their weight and 13 per cent restricted their intake to a dangerous level (Nagata *et al.* 2020a). Non-binary people as a group clearly deserve more research in this area because this recent study has shown that many people are suffering.

Is being non-binary a completely new idea that just suddenly popped up out of nowhere? No, absolutely not. Gender expansive and gender fluid people have always existed, but when it comes to Western psychological research, unfortunately, there isn't a lot of data. There is also the issue of non-binary people struggling to receive gender affirming healthcare, particularly without legal recognition, and the stress that that can incur. Non-binary bodies deserve to be respected.

I spoke with TJ Lucas-Box about their experiences with food and body image.

I think people only assume others could have a difficult relationship with food if it's visually obvious, because of what society has projected onto us. Because of my unhealthy habits and relationship with food, whilst also affecting my mental health it meant I ended up becoming very lethargic and unmotivated to do any physical activity that wasn't alcohol-related. This meant the desired 'body' that I always yearned for (gender-related also) was unachievable.

I think, as well, genetics have a part to play. I remember growing up and throughout life seeing others naturally having a faster metabolism, and it was like food 'didn't make a difference' to them physically. That pushed me further into this dark hole I was in.

TJ Lucas-Box (they/them)

Studies in bi+ men and women

Though the assumption is often that women suffer more than men with disordered eating behaviours, this is not the case with bi+ men and women. Bi+ in this instance refers to people who are attracted to more than one gender identity and is being used as an umbrella term. Nineteen per cent of bi+ women are shown to have engaged with dieting, compared with 24 per cent of bi+ men; and overall, bi+ men are shown to be more concerned about their weight than the general population (Nagata *et al.* 2020d). In terms of binge eating, both binary genders were shown at 11 per cent. There is once again a lack of research when it comes to the mental health of bi+ people, particularly bi+ men, and this is a huge issue when we consider the effects of double discrimination on this particular group. The particular studies used seem to focus on cisgender bi+ people, which is always an important aspect to remember when considering queer body image.

As a bi+ person myself, I am very aware of how double discrimination can affect mental health. Double discrimination in this instance refers to discrimination from both cishet people and other queer people and it is cited as a reason why bi+ men in particular struggle with eating disorders (Avery 2020). Being rejected by your community is such a disheartening and disappointing experience, particularly when you have overcome so many barriers to access your identity. There is strong evidence to suggest that bi+ individuals overall have worse mental health than gay men and lesbians due to multiple levels of stress related to sexual identity (Chan, Operario and Mak 2020). This is something that is not always talked about due to the fact that LGBTQ+ mental health will be treated as a monolith rather than something that differs within subsets of the community. Chan *et al.*'s study shows that bi+ people are even more likely to conceal their identity and feel less connected to the LGBTQ+ community because of double discrimination. Bi+ people experience unique issues when it comes to their mental health but once again, many of the studies are on cisgender bi+ people. The intersections of being both trans and bisexual are not necessarily explored in many studies.

Studies in lesbians and sapphic people

The literature around how lesbians and sapphic women feel about their bodies has often assumed that they are less susceptible to the kind of self-objectification that heterosexual women experience and ultimately have higher body satisfaction. However, there is also a case for the sexual minority stress theory, which posits that discrimination leads to less familial support, less mental health support and heightened anxiety. Minority stress may well contribute to disordered eating behaviours, particularly weight discrimination. In 2020, a study in eating disorder behaviours among cisgender lesbian women showed that 14 per cent restricted their food intake in the last 28 days; however, food restriction was not associated with weight in this particular group of people (Nagata *et al.* 2020c). This shows that, potentially, sapphic women as a community are less fatphobic, which is something that I have experienced anecdotally. Women within this demographic are not very likely to be body shamed by their own community – body shaming is more likely to come from outside sources such as the media or cishet men. Queer women have certainly only been a positive influence in my own life. However, there is still a pressure to fit into boxes in sapphic communities – to conform to stereotypical ideas of butch and femme, for instance, which in turn are still affected by fatphobia.

It is often useful to keep in mind that, because eating disorders are coded onto middle-class, white women, Black, ethnic minority and working-class sapphic people may not be as fully represented in studies on this subject. This is backed up by some of Beat's research, showing that eating disorders in people who are not white are possibly even more common, yet people are less likely to seek out medical treatment (Beat Eating Disorders 2019).

I spoke with Molly Elizabeth Agnew about her relationship with food and body image.

I have struggled with food for many, many years, beginning when I was around 11 or 12 during a traumatic period in my personal life. At that time, my relationship with food was about being able to control a section of my life when so many others were out of my control completely. For me, my struggles with food have never really been about my body or trying to lose weight. However, having struggled and brought myself to a place where I have a relatively healthy relationship with food, I find I have developed an interest in nutrition and the dangers of diet culture. Having this knowledge has aided me so much when I feel bad about my body.

Molly Elizabeth Agnew (she/her)

Across the board, all of these studies mention that it is vital to take into account how minority stress affects the LGBTQ+ community, particularly trans and non-binary people. This is the core hypothesis as to why so many of us struggle, especially those of us with intersecting marginalized identities and no solid support system.

It is clear that within parts of the LGBTQ+ community, there are different standards that affect us, and it is not just cishet ideals that perpetuate this. It is always good to go through some stats and facts, but I am a big believer in having conversations beyond that because one of the most vital parts of recovery for me was being able to hear that other people felt the way I did.

Before I go deeper into my own experiences – and how I made my way out the other side – here are the answers some queer icons gave to the question 'Do you remember when you started struggling with food?' Perhaps many of their experiences below will resonate with you.

I started struggling with food in my teens. It happened quite abruptly as I developed anorexia – I never had any issues with food in my childhood. After all these years, I still haven't quite figured out why exactly anorexia became my self-harm tool of choice (or, as I saw it, self-soothing tool of choice) as opposed to something else. It might just have been what was accessible for me at that time.

Amalie Lee (she/her)

I'm not sure if there's a name for it, but when stressed [there has been] a lot of bingeing and purging over the years, or totally starving myself for days on end and running on adrenaline/anxiety to curb hunger (usually if I'm stressed I'll channel the stress into skipping meals). The control gained over food when other areas of my life have felt out of control started around 14, when school was bad. I used to think, 'You're going to ruin my entire week like that? Fuck you, I'm not even going to eat today.' And the praise I received for finally shedding the weight I'd carried from my childhood was all I needed to keep going. I was never diagnosed, but I feel these tendencies are still with me today, even if right now they lie dormant.

Maxine Heron (she/her)

I remember since I was a child I would 'binge' eat and almost punish myself by eating as much as I could, but at the same time it was a comfort. I was very alone emotionally growing up. As I entered my late teens/early twenties, I generated an unhealthy relationship with alcohol (which carried on for about a decade until 2020) and this, alongside my pre-existing eating habits, created a pretty unhealthy lifestyle. This also majorly affected my mental health.

TJ Lucas-Box (they/them)

I soon realized the reason I was not the same as the other boys was because I was fat. From here, I started my first diet at 11. This continued until 22, an endless cycle of self-deprecating behaviours, restricted eating, binge eating and exercise addiction, which resulted in me collapsing from fatigue.

Stevie Blaine (he/him)

I've struggled with emotional eating and bingeing my entire life. I use food to bury and block negative emotions. I eat food to feel a physical and emotional pleasure that paves over the bad emotions or thoughts I'm struggling with. I don't know what it means to eat because of hunger. To me, hunger is irrelevant, but feeling full and sick is an annoyance as it means it's harder to feel safe via food. In my teenage years, food became recreational. It was a break of pleasurable feelings while I felt so anxious and afraid. But I also believed that eating the amount of 'trash' (i.e. chocolate and sweets) that I did was the reason I was overweight. I saw food as either good or 'trash', and all I ate was the trash. It made me feel guilty and ashamed of myself.

Mia Violet (she/her)

I suffered from body dysmorphia. Until my twenties I truly believed I was very big. I lived in a household where we were constantly put on diets. My peers at school who were far smaller than myself struggled with eating. It impacted my body image and self-esteem a lot but it didn't affect my eating behaviours beyond that.

Annie Wade-Smith (she/they)

It all started after spinal surgery for my scoliosis. Inevitably my appetite went, and through my recovery I wasn't eating a lot because of the strong medication I was being given. What started out innocent turned into something dark so quickly I didn't realize until it was too late. In all honesty, I can't remember why I just stopped eating. Physically I was getting better, but mentally I started to slip into a dark space that had no reason – it just happened. I used my surgery as an excuse not to eat and would drink Volvic flavoured water all day (I can't stand the stuff now). I lost so much weight that my skin was grey and I had no energy to do anything but sleep. I wish I had a reason to explain what happened, but nothing comes to mind. I guess these things can just happen if you're in a vulnerable mind space.

Charl Summers (she/her)

I don't think I've suffered disordered eating but I spent a lot of my early to mid-twenties dieting to lose weight. After a while I began to notice that this was affecting my body image, that I was effectively trying to 'hate myself thin'. Whenever I disliked my body, I would channel that energy into a new resolution to be more committed to my diet. There was no self-love in it.

Jackson King (he/him)

I have always been a fussy eater. I'm very particular about texture in food, so there is a lot I won't eat. And when people tell me I should eat certain things to be healthier, often these are the foods I won't eat and it creates huge anxiety. I wouldn't say I have an eating disorder as such though, just huge food-related anxiety! It's been a lifelong thing. Even as a baby, after I'd come off breast milk, my mum could only get me to eat certain baby foods. So, God knows where it comes from!

James Makings (he/him)

Where it began for me

I have a very long history with disordered eating, and so many memories that I couldn't truly unpack until I grew up and realized how much I had suffered. I honestly didn't know a healthy relationship with food was even possible, and so much of that comes from the normalization of diet culture. Furthermore, periods of bingeing were filled with shame due to the stigma around eating lots. Throughout my life, I have found that people were always more sympathetic towards me when I was restricting than when I was bingeing, and this really shows the kind of morality that is placed on how food is consumed.

I remember vividly that sense of fear I felt around food when I was young. I was around 6 years old and I was becoming more aware of the dieting that was going on around me. People think kids don't really notice this kind of thing, but they absolutely do. The way in which adults behave and speak informs how children learn what is right or wrong. It is the exact reason why I thought throughout my life that being butch was a terrible thing. When adults talk about dieting, say derogatory things about fatness, obsess over their physical appearance and focus intensely on their food intake, kids are hearing that.

I choose very actively to break that wheel around younger people in my life by never speaking negatively about food intake or body image. I started worrying about what I was consuming and what that meant for my body. This coincided with children at school noticing my weight gain, pointing it out, and making it clear that my body was very different to theirs. I began to connect the dots: if I wanted to change my body, I had to restrict my food intake. I started to notice the food being put in front of me, slowly focusing on eating less and less, experiencing uncomfortable hunger for one of the first times in my life.

This was what began a cycle of bingeing and fasting for me, to the point that I would starve myself in the day, then sneak food up to my room at night, hiding it in my room. There was so much shame around the fact that I had failed to restrict my food in the day and I began to get more and more uncomfortable with people seeing me eat in any capacity at all. A sad thing amongst all this was that I enjoyed my food beforehand and restricting it was detrimental to the enjoyment of my life as a child.

I remember a parent of one of my friends coming to my birthday party and giving me a skipping rope because she 'noticed I was getting fatter' and wanted to make me exercise more. I ran upstairs crying, yet she did not seem to think that what she did was wrong. I actually forgot about this moment for years, and as I am remembering it I feel extremely angry that an adult would be so cruel and ignorant. I was 8 or 9 at this time – still in primary school – and the very idea that anyone would say that to a child is repulsive to me. I think that many of us have had moments as children when adults have said something to us that is so jarring to our sense of self, we cannot really process it. Adults are supposed to be good to you, but then you realize that they are judging you and perhaps you cannot really trust them at all.

Being treated differently because of your body is a difficult thing to come to terms with as you are growing up, and the only way I had learned to take control of my body was through food. I think things may have been very different for me if I had been exposed to the ideas of self-acceptance I have found in the communities of queer women I am a part of now. Ultimately, I was battling two things:

- *Being told I needed to be thin:* At this age, I didn't even know why. I just knew it as a natural part of life.

- *Growing up to be attractive to cishet men:* That whole concept pushed me even further into the closet than I already
was, because I became so convinced that my worth was
entirely hinged on that.

As I entered my teenage years, homophobia was far more rife in
my day-to-day life and I was absolutely terrified that I would be
found out. I made sure I barely looked girls in the eye and tried
very hard to convince myself I was the most regular of regular
straight girls on the planet. This went on until I was 21. When I
look back, it makes total bloody sense. My mental health really
plummeted as a teenager and I felt at odds with pretty much
everything around me. It's all a bit of a haze now because I was
so hungry and my mood was so low, but I was a good enough
student to be relatively overlooked. The struggle of feeling
uncomfortable in my body was very confusing to me because
at that point, I hadn't realized that one of the struggles I was
really facing was to do with my gender presentation. I didn't
truly want to present in the feminine way I felt obligated to, and
I associated the curves of my body with the men who sexualized
me. There was a lot going on underneath the eating disorder,
and my quest for thinness was much more about feeling like
the real me.

Exercise

I'm going to talk briefly about exercise and how the relationship
between exercise and food can get skewed. As shown from the
previous studies, excessive exercise is often linked to disordered
eating behaviours and, particularly for queer men, there is a very
pressured gym culture. When it comes to exercise, aesthetics are

usually valued over genuine healthy activity, and I think that is something many of us need to work through. The way we talk about exercise really matters when it comes to finding exercise genuinely enjoyable rather than something only used for weight loss or control. For most of my life, exercise was a punishment: a punishment for eating that doughnut, a punishment for daring to be chubby, a punishment in the pursuit of the 'perfect' body.

No pain, no gain.

Beauty is pain.

Feel the burn.

Blast off your fat.

Everything about the language that surrounds exercise is intense – and not in a good way. It really wasn't until I was in my twenties that I even started to consider that there could be another way, that I could enjoy exercise and stop relating it to restriction and punishment. Even then, it was hard to change the way I felt about it as a calorie burner, a way to be smaller, a way to feel in control of my body alongside my food.

My first experience with exercise in a genuinely positive way was when I joined one of those exercise classes that I'm pretty sure are just 80s jazzercise in disguise. I wasn't very fit and found myself feeling uncomfortable in most classes, pushing myself beyond my limits. So, I decided to go to a class where I was quite literally the youngest one there by decades but everyone was far more agile than me.

I loved it.

I was teased by 60-year-olds who were faster and stronger than me and it made me giggle. I built up my strength through having fun and dancing around to 'Hairspray', and I found myself not wanting to go back into the gym and exercising alone until my knees were weak *ever* again.

Exercise really should be enjoyable. We all go through periods of our lives where we are fit then not so fit, into exercise then not into exercise, free to take time out for exercise then too busy to even contemplate it. I spent a good year and a half completely unable to exercise because of my health and I had to try to build up all that fitness again. That was an entirely different experience and once again made my relationship with exercise very different. However, never again did it become a punishment.

Reframing how I saw exercise was directly related to my recovery, so I suppose it is necessary to get into how I recovered alongside positively moving my body.

Breaking the cycle

I wish I could say it was easy. Overcoming a lifetime of obsessive food-related behaviours apparently takes more than 'just eating right' – someone tell this to the internet, please. There is no one solution, there is no overnight fix, and recovery from anything is never a linear process. Whether you have had an eating disorder or you have just struggled with disordered eating behaviours at different points in your life, there is a journey involved.

I know I'm sounding like every inspirational Instagram post ever and I'm sorry about it. A lot of us are simply used to restriction or calorie counting or dieting in some way. The term 'watching my weight' is an interesting one in this instance because it really feels like we are always watching our food intake, talking about food intake, agonizing over it. Getting over that in the name of your own mental health is a big fucking deal, and don't let anyone tell you otherwise.

So, how did I recover? Well, it took me quite a few years. First, there was getting to a steady weight, then there was a period of denying the diets I was trying were a problem, and then I found eating disorder recovery communities online and things started to shift. I had people to talk to all of a sudden – people who didn't judge me or willingly misunderstand me. Because I came across so high-functioning, I hadn't been offered any mental health services over the years; and even when I was, I ended up being body shamed and ridiculed. Even though I enjoy therapy now, it took me a long time to finally trust professionals again.

Online communities saved my life. I mean this very literally and it is the reason my own platform exists. To finally be told you deserve recovery, that you don't need to suffer forever, that it's possible not to feel fear and uncertainty over food – it was liberating. Then came my interest in the Body Positivity movement, which really took me a step further in unlearning fatphobia. I'll explain this further in the next chapter, but suffice to say, reading books, blogs and papers on body liberation was groundbreaking for me. I began to see myself as 'enough' just the way I was and I saw the beauty in others like me, which in turn helped me see it in myself.

But did I recover before I came out?

Well, sort of. Recovery is a bit messy. The lines are pretty blurred and I would be doing really well on some days and then I'd take a few steps back on others. Let's say I was doing well in my recovery before I came out, but coming out really put me on track for accepting my body and no longer punishing myself because I didn't fit into a certain box. I very slowly came to a place where gaining weight didn't scare me any more, and I worked hard on my mental health so the anxiety I attached to food wasn't so all-encompassing.

As an adult, I finally found a queer-friendly therapist and everything fell into place when it came to my body image and eating disorder recovery. I am really worlds apart from the person I was at the height of my mental illness, but I still remember that feeling. I know how hard it is and I know what rock bottom is. In this instance, the most important thing that I held onto during recovery was the chance for a brighter future.

Eating disorders in our society are both talked about and not talked about. There can be very inauthentic conversations about eating disorders going on that are superficial and don't appreciate the nuances. As long as we live in a society that praises diets and food restriction, it will be hard to have those conversations in a meaningful way. It doesn't matter who you are – if you struggle with food, then your struggle is valid. You don't need to be thin to have an eating disorder or struggle with food. Binge eating is not a failure, relapses are not a failure, you are not a failure in your hardship. If you're someone who consistently yo-yo diets, I completely understand, I get it. The world is difficult and our relationship with food on the whole is quite loaded. I used to just wish I could be someone else who didn't feel she had to watch what she ate all the time. I wished and prayed so hard that I would wake up as someone who didn't feel that burden.

And I did.

Unlearning Fatphobia

When I was entering my late teens, I met a guy who would end up being my boyfriend for probably too long. I ran this line by my best friend from school and she concurred, so I feel comfortable asserting this. This was before I realized I was queer and before I realized that my interest in men was...well, very limited. It was before I had really looked at how I felt about gender and gender expression, so I was definitely basing my worth off very heteropatriarchal values.

We hadn't known one another very long, but I thought we were getting along pretty well. I could tell he liked me but there was obviously a reason why he wasn't asking me out. Then I found out why he wasn't.

It was because I was 'too fat'.

For context, I had gained weight due to recovery in that year, so everything was rather fresh. It was like a punch in the gut and I was shocked. He told his friends he liked me but he would have to force me out on a few runs. Even writing about it makes me feel uncomfortable because I can't believe I allowed someone to be that vile and get away with it. I truly believed that other people body shaming me was my own burden to bear – as though it was a moral failing of mine if someone had a problem with my weight.

I really thought that being fat was the worst insult imaginable; I accepted it as a moral taint upon my character.

I lost the boyfriend but not the weight. A good call on all fronts. I remember that moment so clearly now because I'm furious that I didn't send him packing right then and there. But I was basically a kid, I was in recovery from an eating disorder, I was deeply in the closet and I could not truly have conceived of my own worth past my body.

That was one of the first times I realized that lots of people were not necessarily going to support my recovery but, rather, decide that weight gain was a terrible thing and I deserved to be humiliated because of it.

My weight had significantly fluctuated throughout my life, as is the way for most people. It is a natural part of life: our bodies just change for a million different reasons. It is so bizarre, then, that weight gain and fatness are considered to be such a horrifying issue that it must be eradicated. The language around the fat on our bodies is ultimately hostile and we hear that language from a very young age. Because of the nature of battling eating disorders, extreme changes in my weight became a part of my life, and one of the biggest hindrances to my genuine recovery was the way I was treated when I gained weight. The fear of how I would be treated by friends, family, healthcare professionals and teachers was profoundly damaging. Going into shops when I wore plus-size clothing rather than straight-sized clothing was nightmarish, particularly back when there were even fewer options than there are now. Oh, and then there was being given non-compliments such as:

'Well, your face is okay at least.'

'If you lost weight, you could be pretty!'

'Wow, how are you so confident?'

Thanks? Did I ask for this assessment of my value? Is it really so disconcerting that a plus-size person might not hate themselves?

It is exhausting.

Learning about how fatphobia is instilled in us, and just how insidious it is, is so vital to us dismantling and unlearning it. We shouldn't be taught to fear our bodies for being bigger, for changing, for growing. It should not be so normal to dangerously restrict food intake endlessly in pursuit of a body that is smaller. After speaking with many other queer people – from a multitude of different backgrounds – it is very clear that fatphobia affects the LGBTQ+ community in different ways and needs to be approached differently.

Let's get into what fatphobia is and how it affects us.

What is fatphobia?

First things first: yes, fatphobia exists. It feels strange to have to assert this, but I have had to deal with a lot of people who simultaneously say fatphobia doesn't exist while being grossly fatphobic in the same breath. Fatphobia, at its core, excuses treating fat people badly, and excuses violence and excuses neglect, by essentially treating fat people like their bodies are morally corrupt by dint of existence. Anti-fatness and racism are intrinsically linked, which is why I so often refer to colonial beauty ideals. Medical issues will be overlooked because of weight and there are countless horror stories of serious illnesses going under the radar because of fatphobia. Despite the fact that most people who buy women's clothes are over a size 12, there is a serious lack of sizing options above that in high-street stores – even more so in sustainable clothing. Children are fat shamed by adults at school, fat people are refused service and experience societally approved humiliation from strangers constantly.

There are two main ways in which I personally have seen fatphobia in action. I have lived in both a bigger and a smaller body, so I have experienced the ways in which people truly treat you differently, depending on your body. I have either been subjected to the usual fatphobic abuse and hateful rhetoric or had to deal with the faux concern of people looking at my body and saying, 'I care about your health.'

I mean, of course, they absolutely don't. Usually, these people are complete strangers, and nobody ever comments on the health of smaller bodies. When I was severely anorexic and lost a lot of weight, all I heard were compliments. Even when someone told me to 'eat a burger' when I was very ill, it always felt like there was an undertone of admiration there, like both of us knew my thinness was societally valuable. Any time I gained weight, even due to recovery, I was seriously stressed about the way people around me would take it:

Have they noticed?

Will they think less of me?

Do they think I'm not worth as much as I once was?

Will they analyze my eating habits?

The conversation around fatness and weight gain is one that continues to shock me, particularly because of the dehumanizing way that bigger people are talked about. All human beings deserve respect and there is never an excuse to start moralizing about someone else's body. As queer people, this should be very obvious to us.

Other people's bodies are really none of our concern, but their right to bodily autonomy must always be fought for.

How does fatphobia affect the LGBTQ+ community?

A lot of interesting points of view have come up when I have been discussing fatphobia with my queer friends because we are all from very different backgrounds and are queer in different ways. Although women in general are held to a higher standard in regard to beauty ideals, most queer women I know have talked about a sense of freedom in being fat and queer – like it's a big 'fuck you' to systems that enforce certain body types onto women. I totally understand that. I've felt that way when embracing my masculine side, actively rejecting the femininity I had felt beholden to for years. However, when I've spoken to the queer men in my life, there appears to be, in general, more body shaming and fatphobia in their community, which often lauds certain aesthetics over others. I've seen glimpses of conversations around the level of body shaming that queer men experience from other queer men, but it certainly isn't as prominent as, for instance, conversations about fat liberation among queer women. This is not to say that fatphobia does not affect queer women, because queer women still deal with the pressures that cishet women do in terms of their bodies. Thinness is associated with both traditional femininity and androgyny, which means it affects those of us across many different aesthetic presentations.

For queer men, there is equally a culture obsessed with thinness and toned bodies, which can mean that many body types are particularly under-represented because of fatphobia.

I decided to have a few chats with queer men about their experiences with fatphobia, and this is what James Makings had to say.

> As gay men, the pressure to have the 'perfect body' is insane. There is basically no representation of fat bodies in gay culture, unless you are a 'bear', and the bear thing is also incredibly toxic. The clearest example of this is to look at basically any gay clothing/underwear brand. They almost never show plus bodies (unless it's a muscle bear), and the ranges aren't size-inclusive either. And because these brands are prominent within the community, they affect how gays see themselves and others far more than regular brands do. And this is just the tip of the iceberg.
>
> *James Makings (he/him)*

This brings up desirability politics. I really hate this discussion because it often ends up with people excusing their bad treatment of someone based on their ability to feel attraction towards them. We are even made to feel like being disrespected for how we look is appropriate, when it is not. The concept of desirability is a huge issue when discussing fatphobia, because thinness often falls into the desirability category. I remember quite clearly, as I was growing up, thinking that I could never be attracted to someone who isn't thin – particularly as I considered myself unlovable as someone who was bigger. However, when I actually started dating someone who gained weight, I realized I didn't feel that way at all. It felt like I had been socially conditioned to find fat undesirable for so long that once I started to unpack how I felt about my own body, I was able to see that that was complete bullshit. I felt like I was reconditioning myself from all those years of being told what to find attractive in both myself and in others. Anyone who has actively dated in the LGBTQ+ community will have come across the different prescriptive ways that people date – often being judgmental and exclusionary in a way that can lead to fetishization. The thing with desirability politics is that we are sold this idea that what we consider beautiful is entirely nature and not nurture. If that were really true, then things like body type trends wouldn't exist. We are sold certain ideas of beauty and we cannot just pretend that they don't affect us.

In her book *Fearing the Black Body*, Sabrina Strings writes that 'anti-fat bias in the United States and in much of the West was not born in the medical field. Racial scientific literature since at least the eighteenth century has claimed that fatness was "savage" and "Black"' (Strings 2019, p.209). Strings's book is a fundamental text when it comes to looking at the relationship between racism and fatphobia and the way in which this underpins so much of how we code certain bodies. Therefore, it is important that we remember that being fat and Black affects how queer people are treated both inside and outside the community.

I spoke with Jackson King about the intersections of fatphobia and anti-Blackness within the LGBTQ+ community and how that has affected him in his life.

> Fatphobia and desirability politics is rampant in the community. The combination of being both Black and fat (and trans, but I'll get onto that later) places you at the bottom of the ladder for a lot of LGBT people. You are rendered invisible; or you're fetishized. There are rarely any moments when people desire you, or interact with you as an equal, as a whole

person who has worth. My transness makes this interesting...
Because it's shown me that this is something that is true
across different genders. When I 'was' a fat, Black, bisexual
woman, seeking to date women, I had barely any luck, whereas
my thin, queer, white women friends were doing absolutely
fine. I got barely any Tinder matches. I was basically invisible.
Research done by OkCupid a few years ago showed that Black
women get the least engagement/likes/interest online. And
though that study wasn't specific to queer dating, it aligned
with my experience among queer women. Now, as a fat, Black
trans man, I notice that my white/thin trans man friends have
significantly more 'luck' with men than I do. And whereas
queer women just invisibilized me back when I 'was' a woman,
queer men are more open and vocal with their fetishism and
racism towards my fat, Black, trans body.

Jackson King (he/him)

It is really valuable to have the opportunity to talk to Jackson
about this, particularly as he has had so many different experiences as a trans man. As a white queer person in the dating
sphere, I have found most queer sapphic spaces positive and
easy, which I think really demonstrates the differences that
white and Black people have while dating. I will be getting into
colonial beauty ideals in the next chapter, 'Bodies Are Political',
but fatphobia and anti-Blackness are symptoms of an imperialist mindset that needs adjusting. We as queer people need to
remember that we are not exempt from this.

These discussions about desirability are constant at the
moment in and around our community. One of the most damaging things I notice is that there isn't necessarily room given
for people to talk about desirability politics in a nuanced way.
People don't want to confront why they think certain bodies are

more beautiful or inherently respectable than others, and that is why so many people end up being framed as a fetish rather than a human being. I've experienced fetishization throughout my life, particularly in regard to my weight, and it feels very degrading. I've found my body plastered across fetish sites without my consent, dehumanizing me and making me feel like I only exist for covert consumption. Even when, in your logical mind, you know that you are more than that, it isn't easy watching yourself being framed in that way. When certain bodies are dehumanized by society, deemed unworthy, treated like they are not beautiful or valuable, they start being treated like a fetish. This is something that happens often with queer bodies, particularly fat, Black and trans bodies. It can be difficult to feel a sense of confidence in yourself and accept your body when you are bombarded with ideas of what should or should not be valuable.

There is nothing innate about dehumanizing someone over their body. Nothing. You never deserve poor treatment, and the normalization of this in LGBTQ+ dating spheres doesn't change that.

Even though fatphobia is rife in our society, there are positive spaces within the queer community. The experiences of Annie Wade-Smith definitely mirror the experiences of a lot of queer women I have spoken to.

> Within the queer community, I've had some negative dating experiences where people have been fatphobic towards me; but besides that, I feel very accepted for who I am when I attend queer events and online. I feel very empowered by the community to be individual, and my body is a part of that.
>
> Annie Wade-Smith (she/they)

Queer spaces are often radical spaces, which means they can

be much more freeing and open in general. This also applies to body acceptance. I feel very at ease with how I look at queer events and this is due, in part, to feeling comfortable in my body and how I present in those spaces. I see far more unapologetic fat people when I'm on a queer night out; and no, they are not usually dressed in a beige sack dress from an uninspiring plus-size store. It can feel like there are different sides of the LGBTQ+ community in opposition to one another: some sides that are judgmental of fatness and others that are more accepting than those in any other space I have encountered. It is sad that many of us experience such different sides when, as I'm always saying, we really need to support one another as queer people.

Why conversations about fatness, health and worth are so damaging

'But what about your health?'

If I could never hear this again, I would be a much more relaxed person.

So here we go... I'm an unhealthy person. Why? Well, because I'm chronically ill and my body likes to play a game where it invents new problems for me every year or so. I was an unhealthy person back when I was thinner, and I am an unhealthy person now. But you know what? Nobody gave a shit when I was thin. I have really experienced this weight-health-worth paradigm on so many levels and it needs addressing. People automatically associate thinner bodies with health, and the ableism in our society prioritizes people who seem 'healthy' as the pinnacle of how humans should be. The guise of caring about somebody's health in response to their size has worn pretty thin because it is very obviously a statement designed to appear like it is empathetic, when, in fact, it is invasive and ill-informed.

Two important points to note:

- Bodies that are bigger are not necessarily less healthy than smaller ones by default. I know from my own experience that I was not well when I was thinner.

- Your health doesn't actually define your worth, nor should it. It is upsetting to hear day in and day out that your worth as a person depends on the perceived health of your body. Furthermore, the health police usually entirely disregard mental health.

In a queer body we are already subject to difficulties with healthcare, something I outlined in my chapter on gender. This is particularly true of queer fat bodies, as Jackson King explains.

> It's likely I will be forced to undergo a restrictive diet and exercise regime in order to qualify for gender affirming surgery. This is very common in trans healthcare and isn't talked about enough. Fat trans people are often denied surgeries unless they lose a certain amount of weight.
>
> Jackson King (he/him)

This is where ableism and fatphobia become so intertwined. I remember being so afraid of my illness, not because of the pain it caused me, but because it had been hammered into me that I might have to go on medication that would make me gain weight. This reluctance to give your body the right medicine in case you gain weight is a perfect example of why fatphobia is so damaging. I genuinely believed that if the choice was between taking a medication that caused me to gain weight, or being extremely ill, I would choose illness. As a child, I used to hope I would get an illness that caused me to lose weight. Is that not chilling? I would prefer to be physically in pain, unwell, unhealthy, than be well, healthy and in a bigger body. That says a lot. I am very far from that place now, but thinking about it makes me sad because I didn't just learn that from nowhere. I learned that from countless adults who reinforced it and from healthcare professionals telling me solemnly, 'A side effect of this is weight gain. Are you okay with that?'

My heart would sink. Not weight gain. Anything but more weight gain. A child feeling that uncomfortable over their body changing is something I hope can be overcome. I knew far too early on in my life that the more I gained weight, the more I would be bullied and dehumanized. This is not the way it should be.

There are so many issues with the fact that health is treated like a marker of worth, and it is something I have come across too often in my own life. When people tell me I'm unhealthy because of my weight, I often remind them that I am unhealthy because of chronic illness. Suddenly, they don't know how to proceed. The thing is, if you are health shaming someone because of their weight, then you are health shaming them for everything. The concept of health itself is so complex that it is not something strangers can simply comment on, or even friends and family. You know your body and your history better than anyone and, frankly, you are more than your physical health. Should that need to be said? No. Does it need to be said? Yes.

Confronting the fear of fatness and accepting weight gain

As a society, we need to confront our fear of gaining weight and our disdain for fatness. It is a huge reason why I struggled so much with recovering from an eating disorder and why the constant positive reinforcement of weight loss can be extremely damaging. However, when we are discussing fatphobia and a rejection of diet culture, we must first address the fact that some people are going to find it much easier to reject diet culture than others. I thought I'd illustrate this with a famous – or infamous – social media trend:

The Instagram versus reality photos.

In these photos, typically thin women will pose their bodies for the Instagram photo, then relax their bodies for the reality photo. This is supposed to show that bodies look different in different poses – which they can do and it's an important thing to note in an age of manipulated photos.

At the beginning of my online career, I took these photos, and I know that they can help people with body acceptance. They did so for me up to a point but they can also be extremely alienating to bodies that are still not respected, no matter how they pose themselves.

If you are in a fat body, for instance, changing your pose doesn't change anything. You still live in a fat body which is treated with less respect in your community and you are often dealing with the wider implications of your body in a fatphobic society.

As someone who has lived in a thinner body and a fat body, I've definitely seen the shift in the way I am treated, particularly by healthcare professionals, even though I was extremely ill in my thinner body. I also noticed that I was consistently praised for losing weight when I was suffering with an eating disorder, but my bigger body received barely any compliments from those around me.

This is absolutely not to say that being thinner means you haven't experienced body issues or don't need help with your body image – almost all of us do. But I like to look at it like this:

- When you don't live in a marginalized body, your journey is probably more rooted in personal body acceptance.

- When you do live in a marginalized body, your journey is also about liberation.

So that is why there is often an added layer to the experiences of marginalized people when it comes to accepting our bodies. Accepting our bodies as queer people has that extra layer attached to it – you often find yourself fighting for liberation alongside a personal quest for body acceptance.

We have to confront our societally bred fear of fatness for so many reasons.

When I was young, I remember being confused by the fat on my body. It seemed like nobody else had it in the way I did, and I didn't understand why I looked different to other people. I used to imagine how freeing it would feel if I could just get it off my body, in any way possible. I was so used to the talk around fatness being negative that I didn't even see it as part of my body. I saw it as an obstacle on my body that I had to overcome. These feelings began in primary school and nobody ever challenged them – if anything, they were consistently reinforced. I begged the doctor to put me on a diet and he said no. He said I was too young to diet and my body was growing, but that meant nothing to a young child. All I knew was that I wasn't too young to be fat shamed. All I knew was that every time I had to wear a swimming costume or be weighed at school, I felt panic and fear. I associated fear with fatness, and that only continued as I developed an eating disorder. A huge part of my own recovery was about changing how I viewed fatness. It is very interesting for me personally to look at my body now and feel either positive or just neutral. It is interesting because I know there would have been a moment when I would have looked upon this body with disgust and felt so much pain. I feel sad for that little girl because that is who she is: the little girl who was taught to be afraid of her own body.

Accepting weight gain was like overhauling my entire belief system. I had to do that to make a full recovery because my eating disorder was very weight-oriented. I am sure that over the course of my life, my body will continue to change. In fact, that is one thing I can be dead certain of. Letting go of the fear of fatness and actively unlearning it makes it so much easier to accept your body for what it is and how it changes. While we can't eradicate fatphobia overnight, we do have the power to change our own mindsets and commit to being kinder to ourselves and those around us.

Bodies Are Political

Politics affects our bodies, whether we want it to or not. Society regulates us through many different means, whether that is through structural issues such as access to healthcare or through the repeated reinforcement of beauty ideals that enforce social hierarchies. Our bodies are sectioned off, put into boxes of right and wrong. Even having sex as a queer person has had huge political and social consequences throughout history and today. Being able to have sex with who we want is an issue of bodily autonomy as much as anything else. We are also consistently sold an idea of how our bodies are supposed to look, and that is as much political as anything else. Advert after advert tries to prove to us that we need to buy something to feel better about our bodies, and that we need to change to feel worthy. Films show the same body types over and over again in a positive light, while those of us from different backgrounds are either cast as villains or clowns, or simply omitted entirely. Desirability politics once again rears its ugly head when we think about exactly what constitutes beautiful in our society and how that manifests as disrespect towards people from marginalized communities. It is all a complex web that affects us in a myriad of different ways.

What does the legacy of colonialism have to do with how queer bodies are treated?

I've already written a lot in this book about how politics affects queer bodies and how we ourselves navigate the world in those bodies, but one thing I have yet to go into detail about is colonial ideas of beauty and how they, in turn, affect queer people. We cannot turn our backs on the way in which whiteness and cisheteronormativity dominate cultural ideas of what it is to be beautiful. These ideas affect queer people in so many different ways. Colonial beauty ideals are, by their design, racist and anti-queer. In the eyes of the colonizer, beauty is only valued in people who are:

- white
- thin
- able-bodied
- heterosexual
- cisgender.

Anybody who doesn't conform to that will find themselves, in one way or another, on the back foot of beauty. And the less you fit into those ideals, the more shit you get. Colonial-era laws actively attacked queer people when they were put in place, and many countries that were colonized by the British Empire have only been decriminalizing their anti-LGBTQ+ laws in the last decade or so (Chang 2014). The culture of racism, homophobia, transphobia and misogyny that the Empire exported continues to transcend its time period and affects us all now.

That's the really simple version, even if it really isn't a simple topic.

These body ideals, the kind that protect us from violence or hatred, are unfortunately not just perpetuated by one group. We are an intersectional community and therefore we ourselves can perpetuate these ideals, even if we think we do not. If we really want to move forward with radical body acceptance, then we need to be honest about how our community needs a change. Discrimination affects how we feel about ourselves and our bodies; it is personal and it is deep-rooted.

I thought that the best way to talk about how these body ideals affect our community was to have open conversations about our experiences within different groups. The first person I spoke with was R.K. Russell, who talked about his experiences as a Black, bisexual man dealing with anti-Blackness and homophobia.

I've suffered discrimination outside and inside the community. I've been sexualized, harassed, hated, oppressed, traumatized, threatened and more, just because of my skin color. For me to truthfully address this question, it would call for a book of my own.

I am currently in an interracial relationship. When I was coming out to the world in 2019 as the first active NFL player to identify as LGBTQ, I thought that most of the criticism I would face would be about my partner's sex, not his skin color. Oddly enough, the comments were evenly matched between racism and homophobia. And yet again, the comments seemed to be the worst from my community, the Black community,

> and the LGBTQ community. Off of just one post, one relationship, one moment, people made large assumptions about my life and my partner.
>
> R.K. Russell (he/him)

I remember when R.K. came out publicly. I was uplifted, so happy to see a bisexual man in the public eye being unapologetically himself. However, I also saw this reaction to him. Visibility can leave you vulnerable, and being your authentic self can cause rifts within your own communities. However, there are also the added issues of your visibility and your body being fetishized, which is something R.K. also touches upon.

> A lot of people like sleeping with Black men, but not loving them, not fighting for their rights, not making sure their lives matter. We are viewed at times as sexual objects. The LGBTQ+ community has its share of outright racism as well, with dating profiles that blatantly state 'No Blacks'.
>
> R.K. Russell (he/him)

Once again, desirability politics is ultimately linked to discrimination and fetishization. Considering the earlier discussions in this book about how important it is that we talk to kids about their bodies in a positive way, I asked R.K. how anti-Blackness affected his idea of beauty growing up.

> I was lucky enough to have a strong family unit that taught me Black is beautiful. I've dated both inside my race and outside my race, and found beauty in all people. I won't abide by standards that were made to exclude me. I thank God for a family that combatted anti-Blackness in all aspects of raising me. The movies we watched, the books we read, the TV series

we binged on, the magazines on our coffee table, our art all [featured] Black people with different shades, hair, style and culture. They were all beautiful.

R.K. Russell (he/him)

Anti-Semitism and queerness

When it comes to beauty ideals, anti-Semitism has a very profound effect on how we code people's bodies and our own. Anti-Semitic visuals in society are insidious and are also important to recognize in terms of our ideas of beauty. This is heightened when we consider that villains on-screen are often coded as Jewish and queer, creating a visual shorthand for moral corruption. Dark, curly hair (more historically, red hair), prominent noses and strong eyebrows are all features used to portray villainous characters across media. As someone with Greek heritage, I shared many traits with villains growing up, and it was hard to unpack why every heroic character was my polar opposite. I desperately wanted blonde hair and blue eyes so I could finally be a protagonist. And I know I'm not the only one.

The persecution of Jewish people and queer people often overlaps in history. There are distinct similarities in anti-Semitic and homophobic language and ideas, such as treating people in the following ways:

· like they are plague-ridden, contaminated or defective

· like they are a threat to typical gender norms – such as the feminization of Jewish and queer men

· like they are sexually perverse

· like their bodies are weak and unnatural.

Western body aesthetics continue to politicize and marginalize queer, Jewish bodies, and this is evident in visual culture. We can just look to many of the cartoons and animated films and see how our villains are coded as queer and/or Jewish:

- Scar in *The Lion King*?

- Mother Gothel in *Tangled*?

- Ursula in *The Little Mermaid*?

The flamboyant nature of our villains, their toying with gender norms, their way of speaking... It becomes more and more obvious and impossible to ignore. There is a distinct lack of positive representation when it comes to queer Jewish people and there are often misrepresentations of what it means to be Jewish.

I spoke with Molly Elizabeth Agnew about anti-Semitism as a Jewish, lesbian woman.

> Sadly, in the world in which we live, anti-Semitism is rife, and on the rise. I shouldn't have to face discrimination and hate for my religion, my culture and my ethnicity but I have had to face all sorts of hateful and vicious comments since I was young, inside of all communities. Jewish people are often left out of conversations about activism... While I myself have personally never faced direct discrimination from someone inside the LGBTQ+ community, I have been witness to it.
>
> *Molly Elizabeth Agnew (she/her)*

Our bodies have taken on political meaning, which is always affecting the fabric of our lives. As queer people, our bodies sit in different confines and are not necessarily represented positively, if at all. But that does not mean we deserve to be treated differently, as much as the world may try and make us believe we do deserve it. We shouldn't have to explain ourselves or feel vulnerable simply by existing in our bodies. I know I often speak about what we deserve as people, and that is because these body hierarchies that are so ingrained in our society can make us feel like we are lesser than others because of our bodies. That needs to change.

All that body hair

I spent a good portion of my life being reminded of my hairy, chubby body. Being reminded that it was wrong and awful by children and adults alike. Over and over again I would be taken aback by the way in which people commented on my appearance. I remember being in primary school and girls commenting on the fact that my eyebrows were dark and bushy. I had obviously never really thought about it because it was my body and I was a child. It reminds me of that part in *My Big Fat Greek Wedding* where Toula is at school and everybody else is small and blonde and she is swarthy and dark. That was me. I would desperately explain that I was Greek, as though I had to explain my body away, but naturally, that made no difference to the jibes.

At secondary school my arms and legs grew thick, dark hair. Again, it was not something I noticed until the children at school began to point it out. Kids can be cruel but they learn it from adults. An obsession with how we look comes from many angles and when some teachers scrutinize the way children dress, call it out in class, make children feel uncomfortable, a standard is being set.

I started covering up my legs as much as I could – even when it was baking hot I would wear tights. I tried to wear long-sleeved tops as often as possible but occasionally I would forget the disdain of others in class and I would roll up my sleeves. Honestly, the uproar. I can still remember the way that taunting hopped from person to person like wildfire. Once one person started, it would catch on. A friend of mine took me aside one day and suggested I shave my arms like she did. She also had dark body hair that she was constantly mocked for. We had a long chat in the playground about how to get around this kind of constant belittling and what hair removal options were out there. At 11 years old, we were in the dark about a lot of it but we knew that the bullying was too intense to just ignore it. I was intrigued by the idea of shaving and I ended up shaving my arms one evening in the shower. I hated it. I really hated it. My arms didn't look like my arms at all any more. I felt worried and sick. There was something strange and alien about it and I never wanted to do it again.

I never did.

Did I keep shaving other parts of my body? Yes. I am not sure why I felt so uncomfortable with shaving my arms compared with any other parts of my body but I think it became generally more acceptable as I got older to remove hair from my legs and underarms. I was still sheepish about the fact that I waxed my lip hair, because it felt like most other people around me just didn't need to do that. The process of hair removal throughout history is so layered and I never knew that growing up. I thought I just wanted to be like everyone else when I was a teenager, but deep down I just wanted to be accepted for what I was. I don't think I ever really thought my body hair was bad or disgusting, not truly. I was just told that was the way it was.

Fast forward to my life online as an adult – a very visible life that people often want to comment on. I find myself stuck between being shamed for my body hair, particularly on my forearms, and being fetishized for it by cishet men who think my body is for their consumption. It is an uncomfortable situation to be put in because I think that queer bodies are often only deemed acceptable once they are branded with a kind of capital. Like, 'Hey, you fulfil a sexual fantasy, so therefore my consumption of you makes you worthy.' It is always this insidious fetishization, too, the kind that is talked about behind burner accounts. No matter what, body hair has been something I felt ashamed of for years, through the disgust of my peers and fetishization.

The acceptance of body hair is a very interesting topic when it comes to queerness. Rejecting societal pressure to conform to a certain bodily aesthetic extends into our body hair, re-evaluating it. It gets all mixed up with gender expectations, beauty expectations and colonial views on whiteness and cleanliness. There is an element of rebellion felt in refusing to get rid of body hair, particularly if you have grown up being told that it is an absolute necessity that you remove it.

In terms of my own gender expression, growing out body hair felt like a push back against the idea of what womanhood was shown to be – thin, lithe, smooth women on waxing adverts who didn't even have any hair to wax off. However, I also felt that because my hair was so thick and dark, it *still* was not deemed totally acceptable, even in spaces that accepted body hair. The lighter and more fine your hair is, the more you are lauded as brave rather than unhygienic or lazy. Obviously, body hair is not unhygienic. That is and always has been untrue. Body hair is important, it is protective and, well, it is a pretty big feature of being a mammal.

There are also a lot of outdated ideas about masculinity, queerness and body hair floating around, especially in terms of dating. There are boxes we are supposed to fit into and those

boxes often define how our body hair is supposed to be groomed
– or not. If you are feminine-presenting in any way, there is often
an expectation of hairlessness, and being hairy is then lumped
in with hypermasculinity.

Lipstick and facial hair? Good heavens!

Dresses and leg hair? We must avert our eyes!

Underarm hair on someone other than a white, blonde, cishet
person? The outrage!

People, even people within the LGBTQ+ community, have
limited understanding of how gender and body hair interact, and
simply assuming that people want to remove or keep their body
hair, based on their gender, is an oversimplification of identity.
Nobody should be made to feel like they are obligated to remove
or grow body hair just because of their gender, particularly if
they are physically transitioning. The pressure to fit into a
heteronormative and binary idea of what bodies look like is
detrimental, and this includes the discourse around body hair.

Once again, our gender identity, gender presentation and
bodies are being coded by people other than ourselves. My body
hair does not affect my femininity or masculinity, but of course
stereotypes still affect me – they affect all of us.

It is okay if you struggle with how you feel about your body
hair – it is complex, like everything. It is also absolutely okay if
you want to remove it. Judging individuals for their body choices
is not what this is about. You are not a failure if you succumb to
the pressures of the world. I have gone back and forth on shaving,
waxing, bleaching, plucking, for years and I have always tried to
figure out exactly how I feel about my body hair, beyond all the
bullshit. Frankly, it is hard to separate yourself from the culture
you are born into and I was pushed to remove my body hair from
a young age. I spent a long time thinking that dark, coarse body
hair was a flaw, a 'blemish', something to be hidden.

There were periods of time when I would shave my legs and then cover them with foundation so nobody could see the discolouration on my skin, the mere ghosting of stubble. I did the same on my underarms as a teenager, making my skin feel itchy and uncomfortable. Not only did the pressure to remove my body hair affect my own body image but it also physically hurt me, as many so-called beauty practices do. Regrowth was physically painful, and I think a lot of people with thick, dark hair have to deal with how uncomfortable that is. It is considered acceptable to feel pain and discomfort for the sake of hair removal, but ultimately you don't need to engage with that if you don't want to. You have the power to decide and you also have every right to slowly change your outlook on your body. If you feel like you want to change how you approach your body hair, taking small steps is a great way to go. I have taken small steps with my own body hair, trying to figure out what I like and what I don't like. Sometimes I feel a pressure to enjoy my body hair more as a queer person than I actually do, and other days growing it out feels right.

You have to do what makes sense for you at the time. Don't let other people dictate your choices.

Stretchmarks, cellulite and the concept of 'blemishes'

Let's talk about the idea of 'blemishes'. A 'blemish' refers to a mark on something that spoils your appearance. This is why I really don't use the term in my everyday life and I use quote marks around it when referring to bodies.

A spoiled body. No. There is no such thing.

I remember finding my mother's cellulite scrub in the

bathroom cupboard as a child. I loved the smell: fresh and very grown-up to my young senses. It was too rough for my skin at that age. I was a baby, 10 years old at most, but I had already noticed that my legs were bumpy. I had asked what it was and found out it was something called 'cellulite'. After I found out, I saw adverts about it everywhere – the images of old oranges being slathered in creams and scrubs were constantly on the television. I saw one advert in an issue of *Vogue* on the coffee table (incidentally, one of the formative publications in pushing an uncomfortable style of womanhood upon me, but that is a whole other can of worms). There are certain things that are accepted as negative about bodies. Sometimes you don't even remember when you first knew that something was considered wrong; it just lives in the air we breathe, seeping into us before we have the critical thinking to address it. I happen to remember when cellulite became a problem. Stretchmarks? I don't remember that. I just remember being bought some oil that supposedly got rid of scars when I was in my early teens, even though I had no problem with the rivers on my skin. The whole concept of a 'blemish', something to correct on your skin, something you can buy away, is insidious. It exists as a way to commodify our bodies further, and creates a culture of body checking to the max.

Cellulite

Stretchmarks

Moles

Spots

Discolouration

Blackheads

Acne

Scars

Rosacea

Ingrown hairs

A whole myriad of things that we must fix with money. Is that not a huge part of all beauty standards? Beauty is arbitrated by the rich, by the wealthy. Those who can afford to change their bodies create the rules and we are stuck in a cycle of our worth via capital. Taking ourselves out of that paradigm and looking critically at what we are told is so important. I find that, although many things are easy to subvert as queer people, there are still beauty ideals that carry over. For instance, fatphobia is the foundation for negativity around cellulite – even though it is a very common thing for people to have on their bodies – and fatphobia is still an issue in queer communities. Certain 'blemishes' are also gendered, with the so-called 'solutions' for stretchmarks and cellulite being very targeted towards AFAB bodies. Despite the fact that stretchmarks and cellulite are common on all bodies, I've had conversations with close friends of mine whose gender dysphoria is affected by these stereotypes. These are some of the issues with assigning 'blemishes' to certain bodies, and I think much of it comes from an ongoing pressure to both exploit people's insecurities and focus on keeping bodies boxed in.

'Blemishes' aren't actually real. They are not some ultimate truth. All you need to do is look through bodies in historical art to find that what we consider 'blemishes' now were not always thought of in that way.

Yes, the insecurity is real, your feelings are real, and yes, the way our society tries to categorize you is real. But your body is not a 'blemish'. I will use quote marks around the work 'blemish' until the day I die, because I hate giving the concept any validity.

I have stretchmarks winding up my hips and back, cellulite on my thighs, thick skin that stops my hair from growing properly, acne scars and breakouts. I once felt so utterly powerless over my own body because of these things. I felt like I was obligated to buy a constant stream of products just to live my life. In fact, I did all kinds of strange things, not least having some electrical current on my thighs for an hour which supposedly gave me smoother legs. Obviously it didn't work, but it made me feel in control. For me, that was my biggest fear: losing the perceived control of my body. I look at my body now and I don't see something flawed like I used to. Every mark on my body is there because I've lived a life in my body and that is what matters.

There were no queer, disabled princesses

'Disability'. There was a time when I felt like using that word was a problem, like I had to feel ashamed of it. There are so many preconceptions about what it means to be disabled and, more importantly, what disability *looks* like. I remember as a child people shouting at my mum when she parked in a disabled space because they didn't deem her body disabled enough. It felt like constant surveillance.

The world really wants disabled people to prove themselves: 'You have to prove your disability to us and then we will decide if we feel any sympathy for you.' Often, the only two reactions you are met with are disdain or false sympathy. I think that fear of being rejected and of being belittled really affected the way I felt about my disabled body and my queer self growing up.

I was often told that I was 'only allowed one thing'. I was only allowed one 'issue' or one 'identity' and if I had too many, I was a fraud. A queer, disabled, plus-size person? 'No no. You can pick one thing and that is how you define yourself.' But that is not how the world works. We all contain multitudes.

Disabled bodies are, much like queer bodies, often completely politicized. Many disabled people do not have certain rights over their bodies, and the issue of marriage equality for disabled people has rightfully gained a lot of traction in the last few years (Evans n.d.). Furthermore, according to Stonewall's 2018 report on LGBTQ+ youth, three out of ten disabled 16–24-year-olds are not in education, training or work, compared with 9 per cent of those without disabilities (Bachmann and Gooch 2018).

I really, truly understand that. When you have a disability, every task can feel like you are wading through treacle, and able-bodied people can't always understand that. Trying to navigate through a world that really doesn't make things easy or accessible for you is hard and it can take its toll on your mind and body. LGBTQ+ people also don't necessarily have the support of their families, and discrimination based on being queer adds an extra hurdle to finding support.

There are a lot of genetic illnesses in my family, so I was definitely aware of chronic illness and disability from a young age. That meant I was also faced with the different reactions to disability and how different people come to terms with that. For a long time, I think I felt a lot of shame around the fact that my body didn't function the way other people's bodies did. I pushed myself to my limits on a daily basis and only really stopped doing that once my body was screaming at me so hard to stop that I had no choice.

Now, depending on your disability, this may not be your experience. Disability applies to such a large range of things that it is impossible to go into extreme depth in one chapter of a book. Some disabilities can be seen, others are invisible. Some are physical and others are behavioural. When I pushed my body to its limit, I paid for it because I hadn't learned how to manage certain issues such as chronic fatigue or chronic pain. I never really wanted to go to the doctor's as a child because I didn't want another word to be slapped onto my body. The ableism I had experienced made me resentful of the very fact that I struggled at all, and I then very much internalized that ableism.

This background brings me to the fact that this was another way in which I punished my body for not looking or being the same as that of those around me and in the media. When it comes to disabled representation, usually it is limited to villains or one token character to inspire able-bodied people.

There were no queer, disabled princesses.

Disability does not make you less of a person. It doesn't mean you suddenly can't enjoy fashion, makeup, parties and sex. We see disabled people in the media as either inspiration porn or a token background character – if that. But this is rarely ever our actual experience of life, and queer disabled people deserve our flowers. 'You are gorgeous and radiant, no matter what.' That is what I always needed to be told.

Along with:

'It doesn't matter that you can't leave your bed this week, Essie.'

'It doesn't matter that you can't exercise like other people, Essie.'

'It doesn't matter that you need to ask for help, Essie.'

'You're still a fucking awesome queer person with so much to offer.'

That's what I needed, and I'm passing it on to you.

Discussions on how ableism affects our bodies

It matters that we don't feel alone with chronic illness and disability. The isolation that I felt as a young person was particularly gutting and I know I would have benefited from feeling understood by people who were like me.

I spoke with Stevie and Molly about their experiences with disability and chronic illness.

> Growing up with a disability and visible surgical scars definitely impacted the way I felt about my body. Again, for a similar reason as having stretchmarks, that there was no representation of others like me. I was ashamed to wear shorts and show my scars, for feeling less than and ashamed. It was only in my early twenties that I learned to embrace my scars for what they have given me.
>
> Stevie Blaine (he/him)

> When I first became sick, I hated my body. It had thrown me into this massive pile of shit and I despised it for doing so. I felt like this for a long time, during my eventual diagnosis and further. There came a point where I was stuck inside my home for ten weeks, barely leaving my bedroom as I was so weak, and looking at photos and videos online of my friends living the life I should've been living. It stung. Of course, my condition can never be cured – at least not yet – so I had to

> come to realize that I can go on all the medications in the world, try all the physio and see all the doctors, but my health and quality of life are not going to improve until I learn to stop hating my body. I have to work with it, not against it.
>
> *Molly Elizabeth Agnew (she/her)*

My biggest piece of advice from my own experience is that you need to know your own body boundaries and know that you do not have to apologize for the fact that you don't function like an able-bodied person. You absolutely do not need to accept:

- the pressure to push yourself
- the pressure to pretend you are able-bodied
- the people who doubt your struggle
- other people's ideas of what disabled people are and what we are capable of
- bad media representation as the breadth of disabled experience.

Keep this in mind on down days because you are far from alone in this. Queer disabled people are part of the community, and our access to community matters for our own sense of identity.

We cannot divorce our bodies from the political. The policing of bodies continues to affect our everyday lives, and when we walk through the world, we inhabit political spaces. Sometimes that feels exhausting. Sometimes you just want to exist without all the weight attached to that existence. However, we are also keepers of so much radical energy and we are powerful in that.

Queer bodies are so powerful. Marginalized bodies are so powerful. We need to lift one another up as a community and have honest conversations about how our bodies really affect us in queer spaces. I was once so ashamed of my disability, my weight and my background because I had repeatedly been told I deserved to feel shame about my true self.

None of us deserve to feel ashamed of our bodies because we don't adhere to some heteronormative, colonial standard of beauty and worth. We deserve better.

Social Media and Queer Happiness

I couldn't really write a book on LGBTQ+ body image without writing something about the world of social media. Social media is changing how we view our bodies. It just is. Don't get me wrong, I love social media, especially as a chronically ill person who has often used it for community, but there are a lot of ways in which it is shaping our self-image for the worse. In fact, one of the reasons I even started posting on social media was to be a positive space for body image and recovery, amidst a lot of 'body goal' nonsense.

In this chapter, I'm going to go through some of the ways in which social media algorithms can be harmful for queer body image, but I am also going to go through all the advice I have accumulated over the years so you can make your social media a positive space to be in. You have a certain amount of control over the kind of media you consume, and endlessly scrolling through photoshopped bodies, wishing you looked like that, absolutely won't be helping anybody.

Trust me, if you do that, I expect you to stop doing that by the end of this chapter. I'm counting on you.

When it comes to our selfhood on social media, we often struggle with something called 'context collapse'. Think about it. In the real world we often have specific boundaries with different groups of people and we will show different sides of ourselves. Our openness is often dependent on social context, but that social context is skewed when it comes to social media. We come up against complications in the face of juggling multiple identities and having to omit certain parts of ourselves in the online sphere.

The overlaps in our private and public lives that social media creates have been shown to have an effect on us (McConnell *et al.* 2018). It is also crucial to mention, although it is a raw subject, that living through a global pandemic, in which our only access to community is via social media, has put us all in a very different position than ever before. I know that social media completely engulfed my own life during the first nine months of the pandemic, and what I saw on there drastically affected my mood. Social media can absolutely be a lifeline – and it has been for me in the past – but it can also be overwhelming. If you haven't curated your feed and committed to being kind to yourself, then you could spend hours scrolling through photos of people who make you feel like shit. It is easy to do. Images and videos are edited with a tap of your finger and they can begin to seep into your psyche.

LGBTQ+ communities have lots of subcultures online and these also affect our body image. For instance, when we consider how cottagecore women loving women content is disseminated, we often see thin, white women being platformed more than other women. There are queer body ideals that live in the algorithms; however, it isn't all negative. We are still able to find our communities online, people who look like us, people who experience the world as we do, people who give us space to be authentic and creative. As social media expands and changes, we come across wider communities, more content and different issues.

I have been considering how social media contributes to queer happiness for a while now, often changing my mind about how positive or negative I think it is. Social media simply has many variables and we can find both healthy and unhealthy body images if we expose ourselves to certain parts of it. This doesn't necessarily change the fact that the algorithms themselves are not conducive to queer happiness, particularly when it comes to the censorship of queer bodies. We can find a sweet spot on social media, but it isn't always easy. As we talk about body image, particularly queer body image, it is impossible to ignore social media and the effects it has on us. The first important part of it I want to get into is the way trends and censorship affect our bodies online.

Trends and censorship

Social media really is changing how we view our bodies. However, it also shows us how the world views our bodies, which bodies are considered appropriate and which content is deemed unsuitable for people to see when they open their phone screens.

I have been in the online world since the Wild West of the internet, when social media just wasn't what it is today. I have seen the shifts in how it affects us, I have seen how much easier it has become to alter our bodies on our phones and I have noticed just how much current social media algorithms punish you if you are visibly queer.

If you are an LGBTQ+ content creator, you have likely experienced some form of censorship, whether that be shadowbanning or having your account taken down. I have personally experienced a few different issues online; and when it comes to platforming diverse queer bodies, it is really bloody difficult.

I have had photos of myself and my partner kissing removed, videos about politics and human rights issues for LGBTQ+ people removed, and non-sexual images of my body removed. I have discussed this with many other content creators and it brings to the surface a huge issue: that being visibly queer online is treated as unsuitable by its very nature.

Photos of my body have been taken down when thin people showing the same amount of skin have not, and those photos have been overly sexualized even when they are not sexual at all. This is in part due to the hypersexualization of curvy bodies and the sexualization of lesbians. In fact, in the past, when I have used hashtags specifically for women loving women, I have found those hashtags muted as they are considered inherently sexual.

The lack of safety for queer people online is also a huge issue. Algorithms don't necessarily protect us from the wrong kind of people finding images of our bodies and attempting to shame us into being invisible. They come from the shadows with their cowardly jabs, using all those threats we've heard so many times before. There are so many reasons why the online realm does not protect queer bodies. Images of trans bodies will not only be censored by algorithms but will bear the brunt of relentless attacks. Any kind of discussion on sex positivity for queer people – a vital discussion to have when it comes to how we feel about our own bodies and the bodies of those in our community – will be halted, and this is particularly an issue when we don't receive that education through more traditional means. Overall, social media for the LGBTQ+ community is kind of a double-edged sword. It can be great in many ways but can also be very difficult and we don't always have a whole lot of control over that.

Body trends

Body types go in and out of trend and this has long been very unsettling. The goalposts for what kind of body you are supposed to have at any moment change and shift beyond anything you could feasibly be. I've watched this happen first-hand since a very young age. When I was growing up, the body trend for women was extremely thin. Kate Moss was the icon of choice and, as I look back, very thin white women were all I saw in any kind of media. It was fashionable to wear low-rise jeans to show off your flat stomach, to have a flat chest and natural blonde hair. I had none of the above. Even at my lowest weight, when I was very ill, I wasn't that kind of thin. I just couldn't be; my body doesn't do that. In the earlier days of social media, I taught myself how to edit my photos to change my body type. It was painstaking, took hours, and nobody else knew how to do it.

Fast forward to now and the body types for women are very different. Don't get me wrong, they are still rooted in fatphobia; but artificially enhanced curves became all the rage a few years ago and the changes in people's attitudes towards my body were starkly contrasted. After being relentlessly bullied over my bum and my boobs suddenly... Is this in fashion? Am I in fashion?

Well, not entirely. The fashion is damn near impossible because this body trend expects you to have no belly whatsoever; but it is still closer than when I was younger.

These trends don't just affect women and femmes; they also encourage men and non-binary people to present in a hyper-masculine way. The pressure to engage with gym culture among men is growing and so is the pressure not to gain any weight if it isn't muscle. That kind of hypervisible gym culture is very much heightened through social media and online communities. There are also people like me who are very fluid but struggle to engage with their masculinity because masculine body trends tend to stick to either muscular or thin.

Body trends move quickly through social media, as all trends do. We are complex people who deserve space to be creative and honest, but there is an immense pressure to follow these visual trends into oblivion. These body trends are also, usually, extremely cis-focused and that is why queer people end up creating our own goalposts and our own ideas of how to express ourselves through our bodies. Once I became well ensconced in queer social media circles, I began to see bodies that changed my outlook.

We are fighting both the insidious censorship of algorithms and the issues of trending body types. We are used to looking at bodies that are so perfectly curated and we are pushed to create that image, too.

But we don't have to. We don't have to bow down to pressure to change ourselves.

Filtering ourselves out

Ergh, filters.

Filters mean two different things in the age of social media. They can just be fun, they can create an aesthetic for your media, and they really have the potential to be harmless. Except, they're not.

Smoothed faces on every filter. Bigger lips. Thinner noses. Skin and hair changes. Artificial makeup. Teeth whitening. All in one little tap. It's disturbingly easy to change what you look like but, beyond that, it's pretty normalized. Is it not bizarre that adverts for makeup are consistently edited? That every single photo we see of young celebrities is fine-tuned to unattainable perfection? Seeing visually distorted bodies day in and day out is bound to have an effect on your perception of both yourself and others. Back in my days of modelling as a teenager, I remember seeing the finished photos of myself all retouched and smooth, and I remember being unable to live up to that. I couldn't even live up to myself in those photos.

Fun story: I learned how to use Photoshop® as a kid just so I could edit my body thinner. Pretty sure back then you didn't have to pay for a subscription and I had it on a little CD. It is interesting to think about now because I use those skills to make digital art, but back then my entire focus was on going through all of my personal photos and restructuring my body. If someone else was taking the photo, I would do anything I could to hide behind the people in the photo so nobody would see the size of my thighs or the shape of my hips. I felt a sense of control over the photographs I edited; and the better I got at editing, the more invested I became in editing any photo of myself I possibly could. As I entered my late teens, filters became more easily accessible, but I would say that they didn't become as easy to use as they are now until I was at university. Instagram and Snapchat gave you that ease to just smooth your skin out instantly in a way that I spent years learning to do as a kid. That crutch I had once used reared its ugly head when I was at university because I was suddenly in multiple photos every night, but now I could just click a filter on and feel good about myself.

That didn't really last, though. It didn't last because at the end of the night my face was still my face, my body was still my body and no amount of filtered photos could change who I really was. It would sometimes cut me as I looked in the mirror: sitting on my dingy bedroom floor in front of a long mirror that must have been from the 70s, I saw my face and it didn't look like any of those photos. A friend of mine didn't even recognize me in one of my profile photos. And why would they? My pores were gone, my Greek nose shrunk, my eyes lightened, my hair fuller. All the things that made me *me* were the things I hated, and it was only when I came across online spaces of body acceptance that I slowly felt more comfortable shedding the digital haze and being myself.

People often ask me how I eventually felt comfortable without filters, particularly as I had been modifying my own body since I was a teenager. I try to think of how it happened, how I went from hating the very essence of myself in a photo to being entirely comfortable without any digital enhancements. Part of it was recovery. I very slowly began to unravel how I felt about my body and undo that obsession with every perceived flaw that plagued me for so long. Another part of it was choosing not to use them at all, even when I was uncomfortable. I essentially decided to put a ban on filters that augmented my body in any way, even when I was feeling at my lowest. I didn't want to fall back into feeling like I relied on them to be visible or to exist in the digital realm. I didn't want to look back on every single photo of myself when I was younger and know that wasn't me.

I feel sad when I look at old photos now, because I see a person who hated themselves so much they couldn't bear to be authentic.

We now find ourselves in a situation where we can even edit our bodies in videos with minimal effort. The filters on social media apps will make our skin lighter, our teeth whiter, our skin smoother, our noses smaller. The interesting parts of filters, which allow us to be creative with photography and video, are overshadowed by filters that have a trajectory towards some so-called perfect beauty standard in the algorithms. What we really need to focus on here is appreciating our real bodies just the way they are, and allowing any photo modification to be fun, exploratory, creative and humorous.

There is a sweet space to be lived in that allows us to fully embrace our physicality whilst positively expressing ourselves with what technology has to offer.

What have I learned from social media and how do you make it more 'you' friendly?

Social media is fast-moving. It's always changing, it's always growing. It's not always easy to keep up with the trends and there can be a lot of pressure to continue chasing whichever perfect body or perfect look is fashionable at the time. My advice on that front? Don't chase anything.

Chasing always leaves you on the back foot, and desperately trying to fit in ultimately leaves the real you out. Regardless of how your body looks, you deserve to take up space online just like anyone else. Don't let anyone make you feel like you don't.

My biggest struggle online was being bombarded with images of bodies that made me feel inadequate. That's an easier fix than you'd expect but it requires some commitment. Unfollow anyone who makes you feel like shit about yourself, and stop scrolling through images that don't bring you joy. I really mean it. It doesn't do you any good to be looking at those photos. It doesn't mean the people who have those bodies are bad people; it's just about your peace of mind. When I was first on my own road towards accepting my body, saturating my feed with bodies that looked like mine and bodies I didn't usually see in the media really helped me become more at peace with myself. It also really helped to follow queer people who were being unapologetically themselves, because it gave me the confidence to fully explore who I was.

If your body is being censored online, reach out for help and shout about it. We know this happens to marginalized people online and we need to support one another when it happens. Queer people are constantly struggling with censorship online, whilst damaging accounts stay up for the world to see. Social media platforms need to be held accountable – which is no small feat – but we are up against algorithms that aren't made with us in mind. The only way to do that is to make enough noise and back each other up when we face this kind of injustice. Our bodies are not what the algorithms code them to be.

Be honest with yourself about how social media is making you feel. Is your feed making you dysphoric? Are the conversations on there making you want to restrict your food intake? Do you feel low about yourself once you put your phone down? You are allowed to log off if it is too much. In fact, I recommend it. Social media can utterly overwhelm us, and when we consider that marginalized bodies are so often censored, we can end up scrolling for hours through content that isn't really 'us'.

Being kind to yourself means sometimes you have to be real with yourself.

I hope, at the very least, this chapter will have pushed you to stop doomscrolling – body shaming edition. Social media spaces are weird; and as great as they can be, when it comes to body image, it is so easy to go down a rabbit hole of self-hatred. I learned to curate and diversify my feed as much as I possibly could and it made my life so much brighter. Queer bodies of all different shapes, sizes, abilities, races and backgrounds remind me what a vibrant and vast community we have. It is also important to remember just how diverse our bodies are, because the media will often have us thinking that only one, true perfect body exists.

It doesn't.

Don't let the algorithms fool you into thinking your body is abnormal. There is no normal versus abnormal. We simply are what we are.

Saving Ourselves Through Fashion

In 2019 I walked in the London Queer Fashion Show. When it came to my modelling career, I was never really booked for anything like that because I am five foot four and chubby. I didn't hit any of the criteria for being a runway model in the traditional sense, so that is why I was so excited to walk on a catwalk. I was part of a lovely group of people, and I remember the laughter and the energy so well.

Just as I was about to walk, I remember Courtney Act coming over to the group of us and smiling. This moment is crystal clear in my memory because when she smiled at me, I opened my mouth to say something and not a single word came out. It truly is a stand-out moment for me because I was literally rendered speechless by how beautiful she looked. So, I stood there, mouth agape, as she walked away.

There is no way she remembers such an innocuous thing happening, but after the show I went over to my partner and lamented the fact that I couldn't say anything to Courtney Act. They laughed. I promised them I had tried so hard but no words came out.

'That was my one chance and I blew it because I was too in awe of her!'

This is a pretty good segue into how I reacted to queer fashion moments throughout my life. I would see queer people on the street, in documentaries, in old photos, and I would find their fashion affective, like it began beating in the rhythm of my heart and captured my imagination. This was very rarely on television or in any kind of mainstream media. It would be in my exploration of queer history or around queer people living in London. Being exposed to different kinds of beauty through fashion was necessary to my own growth as a queer person. It reminded me that I could adorn my body how I chose and that the walls that boxed us in were imagined, even during those times when I felt like my body didn't deserve beautiful clothing.

When it comes to my journey with fashion, I think of it as a journey of personal aesthetic and self-acceptance. There are lots of moving parts, but I think my most important lesson has always been to dress for yourself and nobody else. If someone else thinks you look god awful... Well, who cares? After living my adult life online, I have come to the conclusion that people will judge you regardless, so you might as well do whatever you want. Self-expression has no rule book and the very concept of fashion rules reminds me of that grumpy teacher who would send me home if I wore earrings to school. Arbitrary. Boring. Only exist to strip you of agency.

Butch. Femme. Androgyny. Drag. Leather. Punk. Secret dress codes. Genderqueer expression. The LGBTQ+ community has contributed to today's fashion in a multitude of ways. Owning our own look, our own aesthetic, is also one of the most empowering things we can do for ourselves.

However, that isn't always an easy, straightforward journey. It can take a lot of time and experimentation to truly find your style, particularly if you've spent years being told to dress a certain way.

Fashion can be both a radical expression and also something that we consume in a way that is not necessarily radical at all. We may be limited in what we choose because of the size and shape of clothing. We may be pushed into fast-fashion because we can't afford to buy sustainably. And certain queer fashion communities may have standards we just don't fit. I can't really sit here and pretend that my journey with fashion has been wholly enjoyable, because it really hasn't been. There have been lots of uncomfortable moments in changing rooms, nasty comments and unethical choices. There were moments I wanted to be brave but I wasn't, and I regret that.

Navigating fashion as a plus-size, queer person

You know the dress I mentioned in an earlier chapter? The iconically heterosexual one? Well, I should probably mention it again for the purposes of fashion. Every time I think of that dress, I get so irrationally angry, it actually makes me laugh. I've possibly imbued it with too much meaning. Maybe.

My sense of fashion and queerness are so interlinked for me, as they are for many people. That dress I once wore is a reminder of the fact that I just didn't listen to myself or my own needs at all. It also reminds me of the unfortunate fact that clothes are made for certain body types; and without that body type or amazing sewing skills, you end up with limited choices.

Navigating fashion as someone who is plus-size and has wide hips is often a huge struggle. The reason for this is two-fold. The first is that most stores don't do plus-sizes – some of them only go up to a size 12 – and if they do plus-sizes, there aren't usually many options. I see a really obvious lack of genuinely interesting, varied clothing for people over a size 16, and that needs to change. Queer-owned fashion brands are not exempt from this and it's one of the huge issues I have with finding my style whilst also wanting to support queer brands. This just gets worse and worse the bigger your clothing size is, and it doesn't need to be that way.

If you are bigger, you bloody well deserve nice clothes and you don't deserve to feel shitty about the fact that a piece of fabric has the audacity not to fit your body.

The second reason I've struggled with clothing is that the way clothing is gendered hinders my ability to actually find masculine clothes that fit my body. One of the reasons gendered clothing is so frustrating is because there is an assumption that only certain body types will buy those clothes, which simply isn't true. I know people who aren't queer who also buy clothing that is categorized in a different gender than they are because, frankly, gendered clothing is restrictive for everyone. Can you imagine how fucking great it would be if clothing wasn't gendered and we could just pick what we liked? Basically a utopia.

I don't know if anybody reading this has had a bit of a meltdown in a changing room, but I have. Multiple times. If I think back to my times in chain clothing stores, I can remember the visceral reaction I would have as I stood in the changing room and looked at my body in the mirror. I would try as much as possible not to focus on it and to just try on my clothes. Then, I would try to fit the clothes on my body. Usually I would take two sizes into the room, so it seemed like I was trying a couple on, when in reality I was just trying on the biggest. I was so scared of anyone knowing I needed the biggest size, especially when that often wouldn't fit either. When I was going shopping with friends who were smaller than me, I always felt a pit in my stomach because I loved fashion but fashion didn't love me. I remember trying to squeeze my thighs into the cheap fabric that I imagined sitting so perfectly on smaller bodies, my skin slowly getting sweatier as I panicked. I would suddenly itch all over, unable to breathe. I think there was one point where I ripped something off and just ended up buying it because I was so embarrassed.

This amped up a lot when it came to special occasions, for more than one reason. I suffered from body dysmorphia, so it didn't really matter what I saw myself in: my body was wrong so I looked wrong. This resulted in multiple dresses for different occasions – prom, birthdays, Christmases. It was more than just a weight issue at that point; it was an issue with my presentation in general. I was choosing clothes that everyone told me suited my body but which made me feel uncomfortable. There weren't really many options in my size range when I was younger, and even though I was drawn to masculine formal wear, I always ended up in some plain dress that cinched in my waist.

Sometimes there was a sequin, but not a gay kind of sequin, a 'Live, Laugh, Love' kind of sequin.

I look back at some photos and I can see someone who felt so painfully uncomfortable. I was mainly buying cheap fast-fashion that didn't cater to my body or my soul, but I believed that buying crappy clothes would fill some void in me.

It didn't.

Nowadays, I'm a big believer in small business fashion. Every body is different and smaller brands are better at accounting for that. Ditching fast-fashion as much as I could really transformed how I felt about my body because I stopped buying clothes for the sake of it and started being more thoughtful about how I bought them. There are always hurdles when it comes to being plus-size and queer, and finding clothes that tick all my boxes isn't necessarily easy. But many of us can stand to change our approach to clothing and make dressing ourselves a nice experience all around. Don't get me wrong, I'm not perfect when it comes to clothing choices, but treating my body with kindness and treating clothes as a means of being good to myself and others changed things a lot. No more horrible changing room moments, no more comments on the sizes I'm choosing, no more panicking. Clothing is a better means of expressing myself than I ever thought possible and it is absolutely not something I need to punish myself with. What would be the point in that?

Here are some tips to deal with the minefield that is fashion:

- Buy from small businesses who are happy to adjust clothing. This has really helped me as a plus-size person because it means I know I'm getting something that fits me. You're putting food on the table for someone, supporting their art, and it feels so lovely to wrap your body up in an interesting piece of clothing you wouldn't get on the high street.

- Stop focusing on fast-fashion to fill 'that' void. Invest in one or two pieces you actually like. You don't have to buy, buy, buy in order to be happy in your style.

- Don't allow other people's opinions on your clothing to dampen your desire to express yourself. Even if you're in a situation where you can't wear the clothes you want in certain circumstances, you are still you. Even styling yourself in your room matters.

- If you are binding, make sure your binder fits you properly. A well-fitted binder means you can go about your daily business much more easily and it won't damage your chest. Binders are particularly great for a button-up shirt.

- If you really love some pieces of clothing but they are old or damaged, you don't just have to get rid of them. For someone like me who wears the same things over and over again, there are loads of sustainable options for having your clothes repaired. It is okay if you struggle with buying new clothes.

- Don't feel like you have to jump into your final aesthetic straight away. It takes time to figure out what you like and don't like, you might not have the money to invest in a totally new wardrobe, and you might be in a situation where it isn't safe to be yourself fully. That is absolutely okay. We've all been there. Take it slow, reflect, find the clothes that give you that burst of happiness.

Our aesthetic can be very fluid and many of us go through a particularly transformative experience when we begin to accept ourselves or when we are surrounded by more queer people.

I spoke with Annie Wade-Smith about the relationship between coming out and understanding your own sense of fashion.

I feel like I'm always coming out. And every time I come out I become more authentic in the way I dress and style myself. For example, when dating a cis male, I might find myself dressing more femme at first until I get to know them and be more myself. I've been working on this and I'm much better now rocking up to a first date however I wish, whether they like it or not... We're not all butch or femme. You can't tell who we like or how we like to live by the way we look. I can express myself however I wish and my sexuality remains the same.

Annie Wade-Smith (she/they)

Painting our faces: makeup

Queer makeup is cutting edge, always imitated, pushing bound-aries. I feel like every day I see young queer people creating looks I had never imagined as makeup becomes more accessible. The beauty of flowers, the waves and clouds, the bright, powdered neons mixing with the oils of the skin, the delicately placed sequins and diamanté glistening along brow bones.

Queer people have long used their bodies as canvases.

Brushes, palettes, liquids, pencils, spoolies, highlighters, loose powders, sweeping lipsticks and sticky lipgloss. I was once a young teenager who grew up in a time when the intense miso-gyny of the noughties reigned supreme and the general vibe was 'I'm not like other girls', so I actively avoided makeup. In spite of finding it fascinating, in spite of being artistic, in spite of finding joy in femininity, I rejected it.

Once I did begin to reappraise my traditionally feminine interests and internalized misogyny, I came back to makeup in a new way. I didn't really have any of the right things – just some old brushes, lipsticks from god knows when, neutral eyeshadows that were probably Christmas gifts from people who didn't know me very well. There wasn't much to work with, but I worked with it. Creativity does not just exist when you have all the right things; in fact, I find it thrives when everything is mismatched. I used my lipsticks as blush, my eyeshadow as contour and some white Halloween paint as highlighter. Yes. Really. Pretty sure I still owned it from my teenage days when I was going through my obligatory vampire phase.

I enjoyed this creative freedom that having miscellaneous makeup gave me. I tried things I wouldn't usually try, experi-mented more than I would have with all the 'right' tools. In fact, I mostly blended my makeup with my hands, the same way I paint. I still do that.

When it comes to subverting gender norms with makeup, this is where it gets interesting: we are seeing more cis men wearing makeup in the public eye as a form of subversion; the dominant narrative of drag in the media centres drag queens rather than drag kings or performers in general; and masculine people engaging with femininity tends to be shown as them adding to or adorning their bodies. So, makeup, in this instance, is considered inherently subversive for queer men, whereas for queer women and femmes it is often engaged with in a different way. Queer women being subversive can often mean the rejection of things that are considered feminine by default (like makeup).

I have used makeup in order to make myself look more masculine, but it was always subtle as masculinity was something I considered I had to have subtlety in. Then I realized I was still conforming to these binary ideas of gender without really considering how I felt about makeup beyond that. I was rejecting something I didn't need to reject. Enjoying makeup beyond the male gaze was entirely possible; using makeup beyond the confines of gender was what I needed. Drag makeup really changed how I felt about makeup, and so many trends that reach the mainstream have their roots in drag. Watching the performance and the character behind drag makeup pushed me to be more bold, to try new things and to experiment with a queer kind of femininity. We shouldn't have to dim our shine to be palatable to others.

Mia Violet spoke to me about her journey with makeup as a trans woman and how she came to fall in love with it.

As a trans woman, makeup was originally a secret and shameful hobby. I felt incredibly guilty about how much I wanted to wear makeup day-to-day. I would put on makeup at night when my family were asleep and then take it off before they woke up. I was convinced makeup looked silly and ridiculous on me, as it wasn't for me.

When I started my transition, makeup was a shield. I felt like I had to wear it to cover up 'flaws' and be seen as something approaching normal, because naturally I was ugly and laughable. It wasn't until I'd been fully out as trans to everybody for over two years that I started to wear the kind of makeup that I actually wanted. At that point I started to learn makeup for my own entertainment and just to have fun. The reason I was able to do this is because I had gotten so exhausted of trying to reach an unattainable goal for other people that I suddenly stopped caring. It was easier to just do what I wanted for myself and 'fail' on purpose at being what other people wanted, because doing what I wanted meant I'd actually have fun.

Mia Violet (she/her)

Makeup has no gender. We paint ourselves like we paint self-portraits. Upon our skin we find our art, we live in colour, shape our identity. We find ourselves in those small moments with makeup, even if nobody sees us but our twin in the mirror. Moving through your realizations with makeup is like moving through trickling rivulets. They become rivers, they become lakes, they become the sea, they become the rain. Infinite possibilities that cannot be hemmed in by the strange confines put in place for us.

Painting our bodies: tattoos

Alas, as I write this book I am tattoo-less. I finally decided on the specific, very gay, Greek mythology tattoo just around the time the big old pandemic started and everything just stopped. My partner told me that once you decide you want a tattoo, you have to want it for a year before you get it. I decided that sounded sensible and I did. Obviously, the timing could have been better. Unsurprisingly, I decided I wanted a tattoo when I started accepting my queer identity more. When my partner and I were just friends, they showed me their huge tattoo across their shoulders and told me that they got the tattoo, changed their name and cut their hair off in the same year. In fact, when I asked them if I could mention this in the book, they said, 'Yes, because that was the year I started accepting my identity, and my identity and body are linked.' And I started laughing and said, 'I know. That's what I'm writing about.' Accepting your body and taking advantage of your bodily autonomy makes perfect sense and I get why queer people gravitate towards it. The permanency of tattoos and their symbolism is one of the reasons I am so drawn to them. That and my memory of my favourite aunt hating them beyond belief and never neglecting to tell me that fact. I didn't have a teenage rebel phase. Okay, I'm living it in my twenties.

Tattoos have a long and varied history. Did you know that the oldest tattoo on someone's skin dates back to between 3370 and 3100 BC? (Deter-Wolf *et al.* 2016). I found that very exciting. Tattooing has always been a global practice and its relationship to counterculture really changed in the 20th century. I often think about the fact that the older generations around me will still say things like, 'Don't get a tattoo somewhere people can see it if you want to get a job.' There is a strong sense of rebellion against white, cishet, upper-class sensibilities when it comes to getting tattoos, but there is also a deeper meaning within modern tattoo history for queer people.

The pink triangle symbol is an obvious and interesting

example. It is a reclamation of the pain and suffering of those that came before us in the Second World War and is even sewn onto trainers and printed onto t-shirts to be sold at Pride. The pink triangle is born of the darkness that came with the rise of Hitler and the subsequent persecution of millions, including gay people. It was used for gay and bisexual men as well as trans-gender women in concentration camps. Cisgender lesbians and bisexual women were not so systematically imprisoned; it was a similar situation for trans men. However, the black triangle was used for women who were considered 'antisocial'. This would include sapphic women, sex workers and women who had sex outside of marriage. Here we see another example of why sexual liberation is so intrinsically linked to queer liberation.

It took a long time for the pink triangle to be reclaimed and we must remember that many LGBTQ+ people were impris-oned after the war by the Allies (Jensen 2002). It wasn't until the gay liberation movements in the 1970s and 1980s that the pink triangle began to be reclaimed and a spotlight was shone on what happened during and since the Second World War (Waxman 2018).

It is impossible to ignore the kind of body trauma that has followed queer people throughout modern history and why that has had such an effect on our communities. The reclamation of the pink triangle during the AIDS crisis directly linked back to the obliteration of LGBTQ+ people in the Second World War and there is something to be said for reclaiming your body with a tattoo that directly references these historical moments. It's not lost on me, and I believe many other queer people, that we have lost many generations of people to homophobic persecution, and we feel the effect of that every day we live without the elders who deserve to be here.

Lots of queer people feel differently about the pink triangle as a tattoo, which is understandable. Many of us are not comfortable reclaiming something that is a reminder of such pain, but I felt it was necessary to at least mention it as a tattoo choice which comes with very intense meaning.

Now, as I mentioned earlier, I really want a tattoo based on Greek mythology. I thought this was just because I'm Greek but it may also be because most sapphics really love a Greek tattoo. Let's be honest.

Greek symbols such as the letter lambda or the image of the labrys have long been used as tattoos for sapphic people and these symbols once again became prominent during the 1970s and 1980s.

There is also the nautical star tattoo, which lesbians would have on the inside of their wrist or forearm in the 1940s to indicate that they were gay. Tattoos have been used by queer people to be both hidden and seen all at once. They have long been a way to alert other queer people to queerness whilst hiding it from people who are not part of the community, and that is one of the reasons I love them and find them fascinating. The nautical star was a little piece of space on the body where a truth could lie. Queer bodies and tattoos make an understandable match. They don't have to exist to be anything more than just something you wanted that day, but for a lot of queer people the very act of getting tattoos was meaningful.

I spoke with TJ Lucas-Box about their journey with tattoos.

[Tattoos] have honestly saved me over the years (no exaggeration). I remember at one of the flats I lived in (around 21 years old) when stood in the shower/bath, I was surrounded by mirrors and every time I looked at my body that didn't match my mind (in many ways), I felt sick, confused, full of hate towards the world and myself. Once I started to get

> more tattoo coverage, at the times looking in these mirrors
> I would start looking at the beautiful art on my body rather
> than fixating on everything 'wrong' with my body.
>
> TJ Lucas-Box (they/them)

It's significant to consider how tattoos can be a personal and political act of reclamation. When it comes to reclaiming our queer bodies from trauma or an anti-queer culture around us, tattoos can be a vital part of that. They don't have to be, but to look down on the concept of tattoos is to miss the many different purposes they serve.

Our manes, our crowns: hair

I love talking about head hair. I will talk about hair with quite literally anyone. If I find someone who is as passionate about hair styling as I am, I'm never letting them leave my sight. Changing my hair was one of the first acts of bodily autonomy that stood out to me as a queer person. Realizing that I had control over this part of my body was freeing but it didn't exactly come easily. I remember the first time I cut my fringe jagged and wonky as a kid and I came downstairs in the morning all proud of my achievement. Don't worry, I tested the haircut out on my Barbie the night before and she looked very chic, so what could possibly go wrong?

My mother wasn't impressed.

As a teenager, I was somewhat beholden to how the people around me did their hair. Let's face it, I was a bit weird and I really needed to find some way to fit in. It was always about fitting in rather than standing out, because at that age you want to die if someone so much as looks at you funny. I kept trying to change my hair to meet some uncertain criteria that would make me beautiful or desirable, but it consistently made me miserable. I would occasionally try cutting my hair short, but it was never really the way I wanted it and it always resulted in bullying for 'looking like a lesbian'. Oh the irony is not lost on me.

Once I went to university, I couldn't really afford to do anything with my hair and I was dating someone who reinforced the idea that long hair was better. Looking back, I think I was truly terrified of boys thinking I was ugly, whilst at the same time feeling trapped by that fear. It almost felt like there was a barrier I had to cross to feel fully myself, but by crossing that barrier I had to stop giving a shit about what everyone thought.

I continued to play around with the colours of my hair, always focusing on a kind of femininity that didn't necessarily match me, keeping it as long as I possibly could to still fit in. I think I still hadn't fully accepted my queerness, because I was in a relationship with someone who was cishet and most of the people around me were, too. Even though I quietly came out at 21, it wasn't until I was single and out to the world that I felt like I could actually do what I wanted with my hair. I didn't feel like I was trying to look a certain way for anyone else.

Anyway, I went to the hairdresser and got the whole lot of it chopped right off. My hair was down to my waist at that point, so it was a big moment. My head felt so light, soft and at ease. I could feel the wind on my neck for the first time as I walked home, shamelessly taking selfies as grumpy men watched.

Why hadn't I done this years ago?

It suddenly felt so silly that I had spent all this time worrying so fervently about my position with cishet men and how they felt about what my hair looked like. What about what I wanted my hair to look like? Why was I so programmed to think that didn't matter? In that moment, I thought back to one of those pivotal media moments as I was growing up: Emma Watson cutting off all her hair. I remember all the boys at school loudly telling anyone who would listen that they no longer found her attractive. It was such a huge deal for them. I remember having full-on arguments with boys about it because it filled me with so much rage. Even at school, cishet boys had this expectation that a female actress who they didn't know existed for their consumption and they felt the need to lament the loss of their teen crush. It felt weird at the time and it feels weird now. I struggled to fully express why it bothered me so much back then, but now it is obvious.

She did something I wanted to do but I wasn't brave enough. I idolized her for that move. She did what she wanted, she took control of her body, and I couldn't do that. When all those boys were shouting at the top of their lungs about Emma Watson's hair, all I could hear was that I would no longer be of any worth if I cut my hair. If Emma Watson was so vilified for cutting off her bloody hair, then what chance would chubby little me have of being respected?

So when I finally did, it was like I shed so much unwanted baggage. These decisions might come across as superficial for some people but when it comes to taking control of your body as a queer person, changing your hair is often the first option. It can be done at home, there are lots of styles you can choose from and you don't have to tell anyone. It can be that first foray into figuring out who you are and how you like to present.

I asked TJ Lucas-Box about their presentation as a non-binary person and their relationship with their hair.

Once I cut my hair 'super-short'. It took me around two years before I really found my way with it. As someone who doesn't wear makeup, my hair almost became my accessory. Whilst I hated everything else about my body image, this was something that almost gave me something to be confident about, or at least try.

TJ Lucas-Box (they/them)

We don't always think about the hair on our head when we think of body image, but it matters and it is okay for it to matter. If you have struggled to truly express yourself through your body and your presentation, hair is the perfect way to start exploring that. Be bold because, honestly, I wish I had been sooner.

Hearing from queers about fashion and makeup

Fashion, makeup and our aesthetic are all things that we can have very different experiences with. This can really depend on our background, our size, our class, our gender. We all take different paths when it comes to feeling authentic in our presentation and some of us are not quite there yet. Our aesthetic also doesn't have to be a destination but can be ever-evolving. As a fluid, queer person, that is how I feel about it.

I spoke with other queer people about how they feel about fashion, makeup and their queer expression.

I was always quirky. I loved colourful makeup and charity shops and prints and funky knitwear. In my teens this left me for a while when I was trying to figure out who I was/ conform. But as my confidence has grown again, and as I've accepted my body more, I pretty much wear what I want now! It's back to my original style, plus confidence (for example, now I'd never worry about 'flattering' or 'looking slim' as I was taught to).

Annie Wade-Smith (she/they)

When I was a little kid, my mum would always take the mick because I loved wearing pink. I was obsessed with pink and princesses and typical 'girly' things. I think she sometimes wished I'd wear something more toned down! As I grew older and started to find myself on the internet, I started trying to follow fashion trends and ended up having a rather large emo/grunge/pop-punk phase when I was 14–16. This coincided with exploring my sexuality and thinking that to be gay I had to look gay (whatever that means). While I definitely enjoyed (read: 'still enjoy'!) the music of the emo holy trinity and the likes, the fashion was not me in the slightest, I was trying to be someone I'm just not. At 16 I started to discover the world of vintage fashion, and now I incorporate many different styles and eras into my fashion to create my own unique style that reflects who I truly am.

Molly Elizabeth Agnew (she/her)

When I first came out, I don't think my sense of style changed as I was still very much ashamed, embarrassed and confused about being a lesbian. For me, coming out was the worst time in my life and I was ridiculed for being LGBTQ+. I wanted to fit in, so I didn't change my fashion choices or style as I think it would've only increased the bullying.

But now, in the present tense, my fashion style has changed to what I'm comfortable with. I feel liberated wearing a rainbow (when it's safe to do so) and I love a good flannel, which I know is typical lesbian – but this for me isn't a statement or act of activism, it's simply me wearing clothing I like.

Charl Summers (she/her)

I've slowly learnt what works for my body shape, and to stop being so focused on wearing what will make me look smaller.

For years I would only wear black t-shirts and skinny jeans in a desperate bid to make myself look like I had longer legs, and a slimmer body. Eventually I realized I'd got bored with my own wardrobe, and that I'd lost a lot of the joy I had for fashion. Now I think my sense of style reflects more how I feel and what I like, rather than trying to change how others see me. I'm not an over-the-top dresser by any means, but I now don't shy away from pieces that are a bit bolder because they might make me look fatter or draw attention to my size. I came out fully in 2006 when I was 16, and as we all know that was a decade of tragic fashion trends and bad style all round! I think in some ways I felt like I had to start caring more because of that trope of 'gays being stylish', but to be honest, I've always felt any freedom or limitations in expressing myself through fashion are less about my sexual identity, and more about my body image or for financial reasons.

James Makings (he/him)

If I hadn't come out, I'd never have been able to dress in the way I wanted. But coming out didn't make it happen automatically. I was still trying to hide from the world and appease people who hated me so I could be invisible and stay safe. I had to learn to be okay with being hated before I could feel the joy of standing out.

Mia Violet (she/her)

Not much changed. Although as time goes on and (under normal circumstances) I'd be attending more and more queer nights with my queer friends, I have become more adventurous by moving towards clothes which are fun to dance and twirl in for hours on end, instead of what'll make me look most slim or noticeable to the men around me. Queer settings have become a safe space for me to be more adventurous with my fashion. But I still wear too much black and shy away from anything too bold, even then! I envy my friends around me who are unafraid of their eccentricity with their fashion sense. I hope one day I can get there, too.

Maxine Heron (she/her)

I only wore a bit of mascara and 'finishing' powder during my teenage years in an attempt to 'blend' at the 'all-girls' schools I was sent to. Once I was 'brave' enough to try and find myself more, I stopped wearing makeup and instantly fell into an 'androgynous look', which gave me an outlet for a few years. In regard to clothing, at around the same time I decided to just stop caring about what others think. I held onto the thought 'If I have to be here in this world, I may as well try and find me as much as possible.' I must say, even this sounded easier than it actually was. Spending a childhood and adolescence trying to 'blend' and basically be a chameleon – it was terrifying thinking of breaking out of that. There have also been mentions from psychiatrists of 'Aspergers' in the last year, which would definitely help make sense of a lot of experiences and/or feelings in my younger years (like mirroring and blending in). In addition to this, my gender/identity has a part to play.

TJ Lucas-Box (they/them)

While I've always had quite a specific aesthetic that's stayed the same since I was a kid, I've never been that interested in fashion. I didn't become a model because I cared about brands or designers; I did it because I cared about representation, making a statement, and the meaning behind images. But as I've worked in the industry more, I've had to care about it because it's part of the job. I'm always on Instagram, seeing girls who put so much time and effort into their looks and it shows in their content – like they'll spend hours on their makeup for a few photos, and doing their hair, accessorizing, looking amazing when they're just walking around. I've never been that type; I don't have the patience or the interest. I barely put effort into my makeup or hair, but when I see comments of people saying they want me to do more styles because that's what they want to see, it's more pressure to keep giving them what they want even if it isn't what I'm interested in doing.

I've always dressed the same way, even before I came out. I noticed that I got more negative comments after coming out because people thought that I shouldn't dress that way if I'm asexual. It's encouraged me to incorporate more purple into my looks to match the asexual flag, though. Luckily, our flag has a great gothic colour scheme.

Yasmin Benoit (she/her)

As I challenge fatphobia more, and as I lean into gender euphoria more, I'm becoming more playful and fun with fashion. It's a tool for self-expression, rather than me seeking clothes that hide parts of my body. A great outfit that emphasizes my favourite features. Embracing my dad bod/gay bear life. Loving my beer belly and finding it really masculine and gender affirming.

Jackson King (he/him)

I've always been into fashion for as long as I remember and, being an adult, I love the freedom of just being able to choose what I wear! I wasn't educated on the effects of the clothing industry when I was younger. I used to shop for the bargains and the cheapest things and show off that I could look so good in cheap fast-fashion clothes. I'm from a working-class family and that was one of the best things you could flaunt – not having money, but creativity. However, now I'm more educated, I'm even more into secondhand and charity shopping, exchanging and upcycling clothes. It truly makes my wardrobe unique!

Kelsey Ellison (she/her)

I called this chapter 'Saving Ourselves Through Fashion' for a reason. I did this because experimenting with fashion was one of the first means by which I felt I took control of my body and identity in an authentic way. Those first moments buying items of clothing for myself, rather than for the people around me, were like a natural high. I suddenly didn't want to have to go back to dressing for anyone but myself. Accepting your body isn't just accepting your body without clothes on; it is allowing yourself to have the opportunity to adorn yourself however you see fit. It isn't always easy. As a plus-size person, I have struggled to find clothes that fit me in my style but I continue to work towards a more inclusive future in whatever way I can. Fashion still saved me during times when I felt like I was lost in my identity. Even dressing an authentic way in private made me feel like I was in charge of who I really was, just for a moment.

Fashion is exciting. You deserve to be excited by what you wear. You deserve to be truly and honestly *you*.

Joyfully Queer Bodies

Queer joy is why we are here. This book exists because I want queer people to feel a sense of joy in their embodied experiences. We shouldn't have to spend our whole existence being told how hard it is to be queer; we deserve to embrace the wonderful things about it.

Is it not an absolute baller move to be like 'fuck what the world tells me to be, I'm going to do what works for me'? I love it.

Our trauma and our joy can often be interlinked and this is how we make connections with each other. Being able to share in our hardships makes us feel less alone and it can also be why we appreciate the joy in our queerness and our community. There have been a lot of times when I have struggled with the violence against queer bodies in the media. Whilst I know the importance of reporting on it, sometimes I just want to get lost in the creativity and freedom of queerness. Every good, beautiful, exciting, radical thing that has come from queerness I want in my vision. There was once a time when I was afraid of holding my partner's hand. I was afraid of what might happen to us if the wrong person saw us.

I hate that fear. There is more than that fear in traversing the world in a queer body, even if there are times when that doesn't feel real.

We might not be in the perfect space as queer people. There is a lot to fight for, particularly for trans bodies. There are places where we still need to fight for our queer siblings and their rights to live the lives they deserve as their authentic selves. As an activist, I believe, more than anything, in hope. Hopefulness and optimism matter. People can often label me as angry or negative because people who advocate for revolutionary measures often are. But the foundation of all activism, I believe, is hope.

We are all part of history as it happens. And years from now, younger generations of queer people need to see our example, as people who are unafraid of the radical energy in our bodies. Queer anthems embrace our sexuality, indie filmmakers show our diverse bodies on screen, artists and songwriters call upon our deepest feelings, our vulnerability, our heartbreak. Stories that were once kept secret from the world are being told and our experiences growing up are sketched upon the pages of graphic novels. I hope that we can cultivate a society where queer people can embrace their bodies and be unafraid of being their authentic selves in public.

Moments of joy in my queer body

I started thinking about those euphoric moments in my body: when they happened and why. In every case, they happened because I was taking a risk. They might not have seemed like a risk to others, but I think many queer people will understand that feeling of just dipping your toe into your authenticity. It can be thrilling and scary because you've come to accept a part of who you are that you may have been rejecting. There are three moments that especially sit in my memory.

The first is when I started dating my partner. Although I'd been in relationships with queer people before, I had never been with someone who had a similar body type to mine and it allowed me to feel more comfortable in my own. My concept of queerness was so limited to an idea of thinness that I genuinely spent years thinking I couldn't be queer or embrace masculinity if I had boobs or curves. I remember gaining weight at the beginning of our relationship. In the past I would have struggled with that but I felt very differently at this particular moment. I felt like a Rubenesque painting, I felt like a queen who was enjoying the fruits of her labour, eating grapes from an angel, covered in rich fabrics. I mean, quite honestly, I was sitting on my partner's blue cotton bedspread with their old cat, filling out job applications in my underwear. But it was how I felt that struck me. Being more in tune with myself and in a budding relationship with another queer person made me feel like I was bathing in stardust. As I stretched across the bed, it dripped from my skin, leaving trails of sparkle.

Another moment happened in Topshop. I know, I know. When I was a bit younger and entirely uncommitted to sustainable or ethical fashion, Topshop was the fancy place I shopped at. Barely anything fitted me but I used to go in and find inspiration. I remember walking around Topshop and I couldn't see anything I liked. Then I looked over into the tiny Topman section in the corner and walked over there. I think at the time I tried to act as though I was shopping for a boyfriend. Not entirely sure how one acts like that, but I was convinced someone was going to come over and tell me to fuck off back to the girly clothes so I needed a prepared excuse. As if some 20-something retail assistant was taught to respect the gender divide so vehemently they would come over to me in Topman and throw me out. When I started looking at the men's clothes, I felt a little jolt of excitement. Were they particularly interesting? No, but I had a very low bar at the time. I started imagining myself in button-up shirts, low-rise, straight-leg jeans with a Narnia's wardrobe level of pocket space.

I didn't buy anything. Nothing would fit my bum – I knew that.

However, in that moment I felt a little euphoric spark, realizing that dressing in masculine clothes was possible and that there was joy to be had in my body. I wasn't out then but I still knew.

The final moment happened during January of 2021 as I was writing this book. As many of us did, I gained weight during a year indoors. It was an understandable change but it was still a change. None of my old clothes fitted me at all and I'd had a year of fighting against plunging into a negative headspace about my body. I once again had to go through a series of mental challenges every time I thought badly about my body. I had to make the effort to be kinder to myself in a way I hadn't had to in a while. This moment of joy just came as a moment of surprise in which I suddenly saw the fruits of my labour. The work I had been doing for years on accepting my body, unpacking fatphobia and re-evaluating how I wanted to live my life had shown up. I remember just realizing one Sunday that I felt very at peace with my body and presentation in a way I hadn't before. The thing is, I think that for a long time, I didn't truly believe what I was preaching to myself. Deep down, I had still been setting limits on my self-worth, whether that be weight-related or gender presentation-related. I had still been telling myself, 'As long as you look like the way you did at 18, you can still feel good about yourself.'

It is not easy at all to overcome that feeling but it is completely possible. That Sunday in January I had a moment of body neutrality which I really cherished. It was a moment of acceptance, and then I simply carried on with my day.

When it comes to body acceptance, I cannot pretend it doesn't take work. Body acceptance doesn't even need to mean intense positivity; it can also be neutrality. Neutrality is a genuine part of accepting your body, but that too is a challenge. The sense of joy I felt in certain moments has come from feeling neutral about my body; it has come from the freedom of realizing I don't care. After a younger life of such intense hypervigilance over my body, it was a welcome freedom to just not be too bothered.

So let's go for a little question now. Have you felt joy in your queer body? Reflect on those moments because even fleeting sparks of genuine joy can point us in a positive direction. It can also really help us connect to our queer identity, particularly if we've spent a long time neglecting it.

What would you tell your younger self?

This is one of my favourite exercises because it is really hard to see how far you have come without reflecting on where you once were. The fact that, deep down, I once thought an eating disorder would kill me makes sitting here and writing this book even more joyful for me. Recovery was one of the hardest things I ever did but it was the most rewarding. However, the journey that came after that – coming out, unlearning fatphobia, and redefining myself by my own standards – was an entirely different and perhaps even more transformative experience.

So, what would I say to my younger self?

I would want my younger self to know that they were allowed to listen to what their needs were over the superficial desires of others. I would want to tell my younger self that trying to be someone you're not only works for so long and it's not a sustainable way to live. Your body is your body and no matter how much people pressure you into thinking you can be someone else, you can't be – and one day you will really appreciate that. You don't have to sleep with people you're not that into; being into girls isn't disgusting or depraved – it's completely fucking normal.

Yes, I'm swearing at my younger self. I grew up around northerners – I'm used to it.

Anyway, you'll never have a body like those supermodels – and you'll be absolutely okay with it. No amount of dieting or restriction will make you happy – only radical self-acceptance and education about diverse bodies can do that. If people comment on your body, you can tell them where to go. No, it's not rude. They are rude. Tell them that your body is none of their business. People don't have the right to belittle you because of how you look or who you love. You're actually allowed to be proud of who you are.

Finally, there will be a day when you feel at peace with the body you have. It'll take a while to get there but there's light at the end of the tunnel. You'll be happy to be queer, not ashamed. You'll be able to express your identity openly and honestly through an aesthetic that is wholly yours. You might think that everything will get harder once you show the world who you truly are but you will feel a weight lifted off your shoulders like nothing before.

Whew, do I ever stop being deep? My partner once told me to stop being an inspirational cat poster. Anyway, now I'm writing this book, so that didn't go too well.

I decided to ask some fellow queers what they would tell their younger selves.

This question feels like the finale scene from *Drag Race*.' And what would you tell young Stevie?' Aha. I would tell him that you, exactly as you are right now, are perfect. You don't need to change, you don't need to give up a part of yourself to be accepted. Society is what needs to change, our own community needs to change. We fight for acceptance, we always have – yet we often don't accept members of our own community. Masculine, feminine, neither, either or a mix – it doesn't matter. It's a social construct. You are you and you are perfect – embrace it and I'm sure eventually society will catch up and embrace it too.

Stevie Blaine (he/him)

You're a great human! You're going to connect and create and inspire and fall in love with yourself and others over and over. You won't ever believe this but you're a model too! Things are tough, I know you feel lost, but keep going, this world needs you.

Annie Wade-Smith (she/they)

If I could go back, I would tell myself that it's okay if you don't have all the answers right now. You're going to be super-confused on how to navigate a world that isn't fully understanding of LGBTQ+ rights. You'll want to change your appearance but feel the pressure of your environment which causes you to stay in the closet. But just know that all of these hurdles are what help you grow into a proud lesbian. You'll have a loving relationship with a beautiful girl and wonder why you ever worried about being gay. It gets better, you just need to trust yourself.

Charl Summers (she/her)

Love yourself above everything. No matter what you do, who you love, how others view you, what society says about you, always look for new and meaningful ways to love yourself.

R.K. Russell (he/him)

I would tell my younger self that it gets easier; that my sexuality might feel confusing now, but it will all make sense eventually. What I hate about myself will soon turn into something I like about myself. I do not know if I would encourage my younger self to come out sooner. I came out gradually and when/where I felt was right for me. Oh, and I'd tell my younger self to be cautious when in LGBTQ+ spaces on social media. Just get off Tumblr for a bit, okay? The community aspect might be affirming and healing, but there is a lot of not-very-hot hot takes you're better off not reading.

Amalie Lee (she/her)

Never apologize for your transness – it is beautiful, and so are you. Don't be afraid to fight back when people are shitty to you about being different – there's only so much 'rising above it' that you can do, before you've formed a lifetime of submissive habits and you're unable to fend for yourself in times of intense confrontation. Don't take any shit from anybody. Hold everybody around you to a certain standard. They WILL respect you. Never excuse a man's behaviour just because he is accepting of you. Never look externally for happiness – that's got to come from you. Build yourself up as someone who is independent, smart and savvy. Oh – and one day you're going to feel gorgeous, fabulous, successful and happy, and it's all going to be down to you. So hang in there.

Maxine Heron (she/her)

Just don't give a shit. I know, easier said than done. Everyone is concerned about themselves too much to notice that small flaw about you that seems like a huge deal to you. And patience. You will get there. You will figure it out.

Kelsey Ellison (she/her)

I'd tell myself to stay exactly the same and keep being true to me. Listen to Disney Channel. Being yourself will pay off in the end. All the things you're shamed for will be the things you're praised for, just give it time. Those kids who bullied you will be following you on Instagram someday and you won't follow them back.

Yasmin Benoit (she/her)

I would tell my younger self that they need to spend less time focused on how fat they are, and focus more on how happy they are. I look at the time I wasted photoshopping photos as a teen, or the memories I've lost because I would avoid cameras, and wonder what I could have achieved if I'd focused on my happiness more.

James Makings (he/him)

There will always be bullies in life. You can't go through life trying to stay away from them and become someone they find palatable. It's not worth it. Don't waste your life trying to be smaller and dimmer than you are. Just burn brightly, be proud of being someone that's shocking, different and misunderstood. You will be hated by people you'll forget, but you'll be adored by people you love, and the best part of all is how much fun you'll have.

Mia Violet (she/her)

> Don't be afraid to explore who you are, who you're interested in, and the things that you're drawn to. Also, be confident in how attractive and worthy you are.
>
> Jackson King (he/him)

> I would say to take that step to being you sooner and to not let the rest of society put you in these constant boxes for their own understanding and not yours. I would tell my younger self to stay strong because you will find your way no matter what; you are determined and you ARE here for a reason. You are not alone and your best friend/ally is right inside of yourself. You are going to make it and you are going to make a difference.
>
> TJ Lucas-Box (they/them)

I needed stories of queer joy when I was younger. I still need them now. We need to remind one another that we are more than our oppression, our trauma, our challenges. There is also so much delight and levity to be had. There is true happiness to be found in our queer bodies, and there is happiness to be found in going against the mould we were told to squeeze ourselves into growing up. Did I ever think I would love my body? No. Never. And yet, here I am, thinking it's the bee's knees.

My queer expression is to thank for that.

Our body image post-pandemic

I wanted this book to be useful from as many angles as possible, but there is one really big cultural moment that is impossible to ignore: the pandemic. The pandemic has had a huge effect on the lives of queer people and our body image. There is so much trauma that I know we have all experienced in many different ways, but I will not be going deeply into that. The political landscape of our world meant we were seeing violence against Black and trans bodies in the media day after day. Male violence also came to the forefront of conversations and, overall, many people had to quickly become used to seeing bodies like theirs in violent circumstances.

However, there have been moments of light, moments of clarity and moments of positivity.

The pandemic has brought up some interesting feelings in myself and others about how we interact with our own queer bodies. Right now, I cannot say how this period of time will affect us in the long run but I can talk about some of the conversations that myself and other queer people have been having in regard to our bodies and identities during this time.

We slowed down and everything changed. I remember leaving my coat and my hand cream in the office, thinking it would only last for a couple of weeks or so. I didn't get those things back until I lost my job around six months later. The world was utterly changed and, thus, our bodies and the way we felt about them changed too.

A conversation I end up having overwhelmingly often with other queer folks tends to start with: 'This time has been so difficult but don't you feel more in touch with yourself than you have ever felt before?'

I have been mulling over this idea that slowing down has given us space to reappraise our queerness and our body image. I put on weight over the pandemic, as many people did. I was unable to be active and my health was deteriorating. My clothes slowly stopped fitting and at first this was quite triggering. My body changed in a way it never had before: deep, wine-red stretchmarks curving up my hips, pockets of cellulite lightly dimpling my thighs, a sweet roundness around my chin. It was not necessarily the weight gain that bothered me but simply my own fear of my body changing at all. However, all this change gave me opportunity. I sat with my body in a way I never had before. The silence of this new slow life allowed me to hear my body, allowed me to be kinder to my body, gave me the space to trust what my body needed in a way I really hadn't before. This silence also forced me to re-evaluate what my own queerness meant to me. I was able to understand my own feelings about gender in a more honest way, sneakily changing my pronouns on all my social media to see what felt comfy. I grew my body hair out more than I had before, and happily showed my natural hair growth online in a way that once felt uncomfortable for me. When my clothes stopped fitting, I took it as an opportunity to buy things that weren't just safe, they felt genuine. I gave away the dregs of clothes from an older time that I never convinced myself to love, and took my time to choose what worked for me.

Slowly and steadily, I looked inward and ultimately let go of a lot of the ways in which I thought I had to conform, even to queerness. I bought a binder that fitted me properly for my masculine days; I sought out the kind of femininity I had always dreamed of: bubblegum princess Barbie, basically.

There were points that were hard. When social media is one of your only points of reference for bodies and the queer community, you can become bogged down by expectations. The lack of in-person contact, the inability to go to social queer spaces, the bombardment of filtered bodies, all impacted how I, and many others, felt. This was by no means an easy time for us, but I was pleasantly surprised by the amount of queer people who expressed feelings of freedom during this changing time. It made it really clear to me just how much society affects how I perceive myself, and once I was more removed from that society, it felt easier to reflect on myself.

Your body may have gone through a transformative experience in this time, and that is okay. You may not have been in a safe and loving place during this time, and that is fucking difficult. Getting through that means something, and if that made your body image worse, that is utterly valid. You haven't failed in any way if you took steps back in your self-acceptance during that time. This period of time was a huge upheaval of everything we have ever known and our bodies felt that. I know I felt it deep in my bones.

Body acceptance matters during difficult times. When the world is upside down, your body is still awesome. It may change, but your worth doesn't change with it. I've said this over and over, but in the face of hard times, it becomes even more vital to be kind to ourselves and listen to our bodies. We might have realized things about ourselves during the pandemic that we didn't realize before – cue my low-key pronoun change – and that is valuable.

I wish I could sit down with every person reading this and talk about the transformative process each individual has had throughout this time. Connection in our queerness is everything. Just know that my body changed more than ever before, and if yours did too, I feel you. I went through all those ups and downs that the pandemic tested me with, low points with eating, hard days with my disability. But I am still here, through it all, more myself than ever.

And so are you.

You Are Enough

I'm a bit of a night owl. I like to sit awake at night in the quiet and take in the calm around me. I like to drink hot chocolate and wrap myself up in blankets or have a long bath and watch the heat change the colour of my stretchmarks. I like to think to myself about those little moments with my body that are so very valuable to me. I ponder myself, my image and my sense of purpose.

I ask myself: At the end of my life, will I really remember the size of my thighs when I was 20 or 30 or 40? Or will I remember the breeze on my skin as I walk along a beach front, the sun tickling my eyes, the sounds of the waves crashing? At the end of my life, will I really feel happy with the time and energy I spent counting the calories in unseasoned vegetables or will I think of joyful times eating well with friends, laughing, drinking, singing, wandering home half-tipsy eating chips? When all is said and done, will I be satisfied by wearing clothes I hate for the benefit of others, or will I smile at every daring outfit I tried, every bright-pink pair of shoes, draping my body in all the colours I could imagine?

At the end of my life, will I really want to dwell on all the angst around my body?

No.

I want to remember a person who lived authentically, who made choices that were right for her, who didn't take experiences for granted. My queer, chubby, disabled body is a body I am thankful for. Without it, I wouldn't be who I am. It is much more than aesthetic, it is the force that moves me through the world. I will not punish it for having so-called 'flaws' cooked up by cosmetics companies. I will not feel ashamed because I don't adhere to gender roles I never consented to being a part of in the first place. I will not apologize for the fact that society was built inaccessibly for me, because that was never my fault.

Hating myself once felt like the default. It now feels like a waste of my time.

Do I feel great about my body image all the time? No, that wouldn't be human. I'd be lying if I said I didn't have bad days. But they're a bit different now. The bad days used to be overwhelming. The bad days used to take hold of me so tightly that I was immobilized by the fear of existing, the fear of being perceived by anyone. I would find myself staring in the mirror intensely at all the things I loathed about myself, bringing myself to the edge of tears. That doesn't happen any more, even on my lowest days. This is one of those key differences in my life that I only really appreciate when I'm feeling low about my body. I don't punish myself any more, I don't call myself names, I don't become wracked with guilt over eating.

I just sort of go into neutral mode. I stop thinking about my body for a bit. Body acceptance really doesn't need to be loving your body every second of the day, because that's an impossible goal for anyone. You can just feel neutral sometimes. What matters is that we see our self-worth beyond how we feel about our bodies at any given moment, because our bodies will change. If your sense of self-worth is always tied to how you look, then it's ultimately a losing battle. When I feel down about my body now, it doesn't affect the fact that I always demand respect, even from myself.

Bodies change like the tides and so do we. With the passing years, we change, our bodies change, our lives change. Queerness becomes more visible and we are then given the opportunity to be safely visible with it. Thousands of years of queer bodies are etched into art and literature, into Michelangelo's angels, into Sappho's poetry, and our queer bodies are part of that. Even as we walk down the street, our queer bodies take up space, brightening up the puddles we splash through. Our bodies are in the history of fashion, the air of revolution, and the secret letters of great loves. We deserve to feel a sense of comfort in our bodies but also a sense of fire, a sense of rebellion in who we are and what we've been through. We are much more than the number on a scale or a piece of fabric. We are much more than what was assumed of us at birth. We are much more because we change and grow. There is no joy or usefulness in our bodies staying the same forever, and we cannot hold ourselves to impossible standards or the whims and desires of others.

We deserve to embrace our queerness with no thought of those who might try to invalidate us or silence us. Queer bodies are beautiful in all their different forms.

We are enough.

Further Resources

LGBTQ+ friendly online/phone resources

Beat Eating Disorders: Beat Eating Disorders is the UK's leading support service charity for eating disorders. If you want to contact them, you can find them at beateatingdisorders.org.uk or call them on 0808 801 0677.

Childline: You can call Childline on 0800 1111 and they are also available via email. Their website is childline.org.uk.

Crisis: Crisis is a national charity tackling homelessness in the UK. They can be found at crisis.org.uk. Their phone number is 0300 636 1967.

Exist Loudly: Exist Loudly is an organization founded by Tanya Compas and is committed to making safe spaces for young queer, Black people. Exist Loudly can be found at @existloudly on Instagram and @existloudlyuk on Twitter.

LGBT Foundation: LGBT Foundation offers a range of support for LGBT communities and can be found online at lgbt.foundation.

Mermaids: Mermaids support transgender and gender variant children and can be found at mermaidsuk.org.uk. They also support families of transgender families.

The Mix: The Mix is the UK's leading support service for people between 13 and 25 years old. Their website is themix.org.uk and there you can find all the information to contact them. Their number is 0808 808 4994.

NEDA: NEDA is the National Eating Disorders Association in the USA. They can be contacted at nationaleatingdisorders.org or +1-800-931-2237.

Switchboard LGBT+ Hotline: Switchboard LGBT+ is a national hotline in the UK and you can call them on 0300 330 0630. There is also the option to live chat or text them.

Useful books for body image and LGBTQ+ issues

Am I Ugly? by Michelle Elman (Anima, 2019)

Bi the Way by Lo Shearing (Jessica Kingsley Publishers, 2021)

Body Happy Kids by Molly Forbes (Vermilion, 2021)

Body Positive Power by Megan Jayne Crabbe (Vermilion, 2017)

Fat and Queer by Bruce Owens Grimm, Miguel Morales and Tiff Ferentini (Jessica Kingsley Publishers, 2021)

Food Isn't Medicine by Dr Joshua Woolrich (Vermilion, 2021)

In Their Shoes by Jamie Windust (Jessica Kingsley Publishers, 2020)

Trans Power by Juno Roche (Jessica Kingsley Publishers, 2019)

References

Albert Kennedy Trust (2015) *LGBT Youth Homelessness: A UK National Scoping of Cause, Prevalence, Response and Outcome*. Available at www.theproudtrust.org/resources/research-and-guidance-by-other-organisations/lgbt-youth-homelessness-a-uk-national-scoping-of-cause-prevalence-response-and-outcome, accessed 5 June 2021.

Anorexia Bulimia Care (n.d.) *About Eating Disorders: Statistics*. Available at www.anorexiabulimiacare.org.uk/about/statistics, accessed 5 June 2021.

Avery, D. (2020) 'Bisexual men more prone to eating disorders than gay or straight men, study finds.' *NBC News*. Available at www.nbcnews.com/feature/nbc-out/bisexual-men-more-prone-eating-disorders-gay-or-straight-men-n1251626, accessed 5 June 2021.

Bachmann, C.L. & Gooch, B. (2018) *LGBT in Britain Health Report*. Stonewall. Available at www.stonewall.org.uk/system/files/lgbt_in_britain_health.pdf, accessed 5 June 2021.

Beat Eating Disorders (2019) 'New research shows eating disorder stereotypes prevent people finding help.' Available at https://www.beateatingdisorders.org.uk/news/beat-news/eating-disorder-stereotypes-prevent-help, accessed 7 October 2021.

Butler, J. (2004) *Undoing Gender*. Abingdon: Routledge.

Chan, R.C.H., Operario, D. & Mak, W.W.S. (2020) 'Bisexual individuals are at greater risk of poor mental health than lesbians and gay men: The mediating role of sexual identity stress at multiple levels.' *Journal of Affective Disorders* 260, 292–301.

Chang, S. (2014) 'The Postcolonial Problem for Global Gay Rights.' *Scholarly Works* 1109. Available at https://scholars.law.unlv.edu/facpub/1109, accessed 5 June 2021.

Chapman L. (1998) 'Body image and HIV: Implications for support and care.' *AIDS Care* 10(2), 179–187.

Deter-Wolf, A., Robitaille, B. Krutak, L. & Galliot, S. (2016) 'The world's oldest tattoos.' *Journal of Archaeological Science: Reports* 5, 19–24. Available at https://doi.org/10.1016/j.jasrep.2015.11.007, accessed 5 June 2021.

Evans, D. (n.d.) *Marriage Equality*. Center for Disability Rights. Available at www.cdrnys.org/blog/disability-dialogue/the-disability-dialogue-marriage-equality, accessed 5 June 2021.

Jensen, E.N. (2002) 'The pink triangle and political consciousness: Gays, lesbians, and the memory of Nazi persecution.' *Journal of the History of Sexuality* 11(1–2), 319–349. Available at www.jstor.org/stable/3704560, accessed 5 June 2021.

McCallum Place (2020) *Why Transgender People Are More Likely to Develop an Eating Disorder*. Eating Disorder Hope. Available at www.eatingdisorderhope.com/blog/transgender-people-likely-develop-eating-disorder, accessed 5 June 2021.

McConnell, E., Néray, B., Hogan, B., Korpak, A., Clifford, A. & Birkett, M. (2018) '"Everybody puts their whole life on Facebook": Identity management and the online social networks of LGBTQ youth.' *International Journal of Environmental Research and Public Health* 15(6), 1078. Available at www.ncbi.nlm.nih.gov/pmc/articles/PMC6025558, accessed 5 June 2021.

Nagata, J.M., Capriotti, M.R., Murray, S.B., Compte, E.J. *et al.* (2019) 'Community norms for the Eating Disorder Examination Questionnaire among cisgender gay men.' *European Eating Disorders Review* 28(1), 92–101. Available at https://doi.org/10.1002/erv.2708, accessed 5 June 2021.

Nagata, J.M., Compte, E.J., Cattle, C.J., Flentje, A. *et al.* (2020a) 'Community norms for the Eating Disorder Examination Questionnaire (EDE-Q) among gender-expansive populations.' *Journal of Eating Disorders* 8(74). Available at https://jeatdisord.biomedcentral.com/articles/10.1186/s40337-020-00352-x, accessed 5 June 2021.

Nagata, J.M., Murray, S.B., Compte, E.J., Pak, E.H. *et al.* (2020b) 'Community norms for the Eating Disorder Examination Questionnaire (EDE-Q) among transgender men and women.' *Eating Behaviors* 37. Available at doi.org/10.1016/j.eatbeh.2020.101381, accessed 5 June 2021.

Nagata, J.M., Murray, S.B., Flentje, A., Compte, E.J. *et al.* (2020c) 'Eating disorder attitudes and disordered eating behaviors as measured by the Eating Disorder Examination Questionnaire (EDE-Q) among cisgender lesbian women.' *Body Image* 34, 215–220. Available at https://doi.org/10.1016/j.bodyim.2020.06.005, accessed 5 June 2021.

Nagata, J.M., Compte, E.J., Murray, S.B., Schauer, R. *et al.* (2020d) 'Community norms for the eating disorder examination questionnaire (EDE-Q) among cisgender bisexual plus women and men.' *Eating and Weight Disorders*. Available at doi.org/10.1007/s40519-020-01070-8, accessed 15 June 2021.

NEDA (2021) *Eating Disorders in LGBTQ+ Populations*. Available at www.nationaleatingdisorders.org/learn/general-information/lgbtq, accessed 5 June 2021.

PRIDE Study (2017) 'The PRIDE Study.' Available at https://pridestudy.org, accessed 5 June 2021.

Rawlings, Z. (2016) *Body Dysmorphic Disorder in Gay Males*. Eating Disorder Recovery Centre. Available at www.eatingrecoverycenter. com/blog/signs-symptoms/Body-Dysmorphic-Disorder-in-Gay-Males, accessed 5 June 2021.

Ru Paul (2017) *Ru Paul's Drag Race*: Season 9, Episode 5: 'Good Morning Bitches'. World of Wonder (21 April).

Stonewall (2018) *LGBT in Britain – Health Report*. Available at www. stonewall.org.uk/system/files/lgbt_in_britain_health.pdf, accessed 29 June 2021.

Strings, S. (2019) *Fearing the Black Body: The Racial Origins of Fat Phobia*. New York, NY: New York University Press.

Waxman, O.B. (2018) 'How the Nazi regime's pink triangle symbol was repurposed for LGBTQ Pride. *TIME* (31 May, 2018). Available at https://time.com/5295476/gay-pride-pink-triangle-history, accessed 5 June 2021.

Zucker, T. (2018) *Eating Disorders vs. Disordered Eating: What's the Difference?* NEDA. Available at www.nationaleatingdisorders. org/blog/eating-disorders-versus-disordered-eating, accessed 5 June 2021.

Index

ableism
  affecting bodies 153–5
  intertwined with fatphobia 131–2
  trigger warning 11
activism 17, 60, 142, 192
advice for younger self 195–200
ageing 70–2
Agnew, Molly Elizabeth 52, 91,
  109–10, 142, 153–4, 186
AIDS crisis 40, 62, 71, 180
Albert Kennedy Trust 42
anorexia 14, 97, 98, 110
Anorexia Bulimia Care 97
anti-Semitism 141–3
asexuality 57, 58, 63–4, 74, 189
Avery, D. 108

Bachmann, C.L. 151
Beat Eating Disorders 109, 209
Benoit, Yasmin 32, 50, 63–4, 74,
  188–9, 199
bi+ men and women 107–8
bisexuality 19, 57–8, 65, 74, 139–40,
  180
black triangle 180

Blaine, Stevie 30–1, 51, 73, 111–12,
  153, 197
'blemishes' 147–50
body
  awareness of 25–6
  challenging negative feelings
    about 52–4
  childhood experiences of 25–34
  compartmentalization 28
  different experiences 36–7
  feeling good in 34–6
  feeling uncomfortable in 29–34
  joyfully queer 191–203
  LGBTQ+ community and gender
    norms 80–3
  see also politics of body
body acceptance
  and clothes 190
  end of life imaginings 205–6
  fighting for liberation alongside
    134
  as important during difficult
    times 203
  nature of 36
  and neutrality 190, 206–7
  in online spaces 164

body acceptance *cont.*
    as part of Body Positivity 21, 22
    sexuality informing 65–70, 72, 74,
        75, 92
body boundaries 28, 79–80, 86, 154
body checking 53, 148
body dissociation/disconnection
    45–6, 48, 86
body dysmorphia 41, 82, 112, 173
body hair 143–7, 202
body image
    and body hair 147, 184–5
    causes of feeling bad about 40–2
    experiences of feeling confident
        in 50–2
    and experiences with food 105,
        106–7, 109, 112, 114
    of gay men 102–3
    and gender 87–94
    gender euphoria linked to 82
    opening up dialogue on 16–17, 20
    post-pandemic 200–3
    and sexuality 14, 54, 60–5, 72–5
    and social media 157, 158–9, 166
    useful books 210–11
body neutrality 36, 134, 195, 206–7
Body Positivity 20, 21–2, 36, 43, 60,
    79, 118–19
body reclamation
    causes of body image negativity
        40–2
    cultural battlegrounds 39–40
    experiences of 50–4
    healing 45–6
    periods of bodily suffering 42–5
    self-care 46–8
    self-reflection 48–50
body shaming 39, 60, 109, 121–2, 125,
    160
body trends 161–2
bullying 34, 41, 50, 68, 100, 144, 199
Butler, J. 77–9

capitalism 15, 149
cellulite 36, 147–50
censorship 159–60, 162, 166
Chang, S. 61, 138–9
Chan, R.C.H. 108
Chapman, L. 62
Childline 209
'chosen family' 49
chronic illness 20, 44–5, 132, 151,
    153–4
cisgender gay men 102–3
cisgender lesbian women 108–9, 180
cishet (cisgender and heterosexual)
    15
class 21, 40, 43–4, 109, 190
clothing
    blue dress and gender 87–8
    comfortable 47, 53
    experiences of 185–90, 193–4
    to fit self 35–6, 202
    for gender euphoria 47, 82–3
    issues with 171–5
    sizing options 124, 171–2
colonialism 128, 138–41, 145, 155
coming out
    and fashion 175, 187, 189
    negative aspects 54, 56, 58–9,
        139–40, 186, 189
    as ongoing process 56–7, 175
    positive aspects 58–9, 72, 74, 119,
        187
    pressures of 57–8
competition 66–7
'context collapse' 158
Couleé, S. 98, 100
Crisis 209
cultural battlegrounds 39–40
cultural obsessions
    with ageing 71
    with thinness 14

desirability politics 126–9, 137–8,
    140–1

Deter-Wolf, A. 179
disability 21, 44–5, 150–5
discrimination 13, 96, 107–8, 139–40, 142
disordered eating
  anxiety and depression often linked to 102
  bi+ men and women 107
  breaking cycle of 118–20
  vs eating disorders 95–6
  excessive exercise linked to 116
  minority stress contributing to 108
  recurrence during stressful periods 101
  shame around 99–100
  shaping adolescence 15
  societal approval of 99
  trans people suffering exponentially with 104
doomscrolling 166
double discrimination 107–8

eating disorders
  affecting LGBTQ+ community 15, 96–7, 101–16
  and body dysmorphia 82
  breaking cycle of 118–20
  vs disordered eating 95–6
  and grief 78
  and lack of resources 44
  as mental illness 18, 97
  as most likely to form during adolescence 97
  occurring in childhood 14, 114
  perceptions of 97–9
  as preventing living a good life 17–18
  trigger warning 11
Ellison, Kelsey 30, 72, 189–90, 199
euphoria 49, 56, 82–3, 189
Evans, D. 151

exercise
  excessive 102, 104, 111
  reframing perception of 116–17
Exist Loudly 209

fashion
  background and context 169–71
  experiences 185–90
  hair 182–5
  makeup 176–7
  navigating as plus-size, queer person 171–5
  as saviour 190
  tattoos 178–82
fatness
  anti-fat bias 103, 123, 127
  confronting fear of 132–5
  damaging conversations about 130–2
  hostile language around 114, 122, 124–5
fatphobia
  background and context 121–3
  and body image 41
  changing mindsets 135
  and eating disorders in cisgender gay men 102–3
  intertwined with ableism 131–2
  and LGBTQ+ community 125–30
  nature of 123–5
  and negativity around cellulite 149
  trigger warning 11
femininity
  exploring 92
  and hair 183
  and makeup 176–7
  performing 88, 89
  and personal value 61
  pressure to conform to 81, 89, 91–2
  rejection of 91–2, 125, 176
  seeking out 202
  thinness associated with 125

feminist theory 60, 77–8
films 103, 137, 142, 143, 192
filters 162–5
fluidity 26, 27, 48, 56, 65, 88–9, 93, 175
food
    complex relationship with 95–6,
        98, 120
    and exercise 116–17
    experiences of struggles with 14,
        17, 110–16
    see also disordered eating; eating
        disorders

gender
    and body image 87–94
    and healthcare 81, 83–7
    overview 77–80
gender dysphoria 13, 41, 81–2, 90, 149
gender euphoria 82–3, 189
gender expansive/non-binary
    people 105–6
gender norms
    affecting how LGBTQ+
        community feel about their
        bodies 80–3
    and anti-Semitism 141–2
    subverting with makeup 177
genetics 107, 151
Gooch, B. 151
grief 78–9

hair
    body 143–7, 202
    head 182–5
healing 45–6
health 130–2
    see also mental health
healthcare
    and gender 81, 83–7
    lack of appropriate 41, 106
    for queer fat bodies 131
Heron, Maxine 33, 51, 61–2, 84, 91,
    104–5, 110–11, 187–8, 198

heteronormativity 26, 61–2, 138
heteropatriarchy 26, 28, 58, 79, 121
heterosexuality
    as considered innate 75
    and eating disorder 102
    life rigidly structured by 57
    re-evaluating 60–5
homelessness 42, 209
homophobia 41, 66, 115, 139–40

imperialism 61, 128
Instagram 18–19, 50–1, 133, 163, 189
'inviting people in' 56, 58

Jensen, E.N. 180
joy, moments of 192–5, 205
    see also queer joy

King, Jackson 30, 85–6, 90, 113, 127–8,
    131, 189, 200

labels 70
Lee, Amalie 34, 74, 110–11, 198
lesbians
    eating disorders 108–9
    nautical star tattoo 181
    sexualization of 160
LGBT Foundation 210
LGBTQ+ community
    contribution to fashion 170
    and disability 151
    eating disorders affecting 15,
        96–7, 101–16
    fatphobia affecting 125–30
    fear of ageing as detrimental to
        70–5
    first awareness of feeling
        uncomfortable in body 29–34
    gender norms affecting feelings
        about body 80–3
    homelessness as issue for 42
    online censorship 159–60
    online/phone resources 209–10

online subcultures 158-9
racism within 140, 142
useful books 210-11
in wartime 180
Lucas-Box, T.J. 33, 84-5, 92-3, 106-7,
111, 181-2, 184-5, 188, 200

makeup
edited adverts for 162-3
experiences of 185-90
painting faces 176-8
self care 47
used for cover, not enjoyment 13
Makings, James 33-4, 50-1, 72-3,
102-3, 113, 126, 186-7, 199
Mak, W.W.S. 108
McCallum Place 104
McConnell, E. 158
mental health
aim to open up dialogue about
16-17
based on minority stress 15, 40
of bi+ people 107-8
as cause of negative body image
41
double discrimination affecting
107-8
gender dysphoria and body
dysmorphia 81-2
lack of support for 18-19, 104
limited studies into LGBTQ+ 102
of older LGBTQ+ people 71
sexual orientation affecting 54
stressors 97
teenage struggles with 14-15, 116
toll of discrimination 13
Mermaids 210
minority stress 15, 40, 104, 108, 110
The Mix 210

Nagata, J.M. 15, 102, 104, 106, 107,
108-9

NEDA (US National Eating
Disorders Association) 96, 210

online communities
gym culture heightened through
161
as saviour 15, 118
see also social media
openness 49, 78, 158
Operario, D. 108

pandemic 158, 200-3
pink triangle 179-81
politics of body
ableism affecting bodies 153-5
anti-Semitism and queerness
141-3
body hair 143-7
colonialism legacy 138-41
context 137-8
disability 150-5
stretchmarks, cellulite and
'blemishes' 147-50
see also desirability politics
positivity 50-1, 53
poverty 43-4
predator stereotype 63, 66
prettiness 67
PRIDE Study 101-2

queer joy 13, 41, 191, 200
queer liberation 20, 79, 180
queerness
and anti-Semitism 141-3
appreciating joy in 191
being open about 78
coming to terms with 65-6
as comprising many things 20
connection in 203
as defined by self 56
diversity in 70
embracing 59, 70, 191, 207
linked to sense of fashion 171

queerness *cont.*
  lived realities of 13
  as opening doors to self-
    expression 61
  pandemic allowing reappraisal
    of 201–2
  power in 28
queer representation 67
queer self-acceptance 28

racism
  as cause of negative body image
    41
  experiences of 139–41
  interlinked with anti-fatness
    123, 127
  trigger warning 12
Rawlings, Z. 60
reflection *see* self-reflection
Ru Paul 98
Russell, R.K. 29, 51, 92, 139–41, 198

sapphic people
  eating disorders 108–9
  as feeling slightly predatory 66
  tattoos 180, 181
self-care 45–8
selfies 51–2, 183
self-image 15, 17, 33, 41, 65, 157
self-love 13–14, 37, 45
self-reflection 48–50, 94
sex positivity 64, 160
sexuality
  and body image 14, 54, 60–5, 72–5
  coming out 56–60
  context 55–6
  feelings of guilt or shame over 41
  informing body acceptance
    65–70, 72, 74, 75, 92
  queer anthems embracing 192
sexual orientation 54, 55, 62, 75
shame
  around disability 151, 155

around food and eating 96, 98–9,
    100, 114
  internalized 65
  over body image 32
  over sexuality 41, 66
  see also body shaming
simmering pot analogy 27
social media
  'context collapse' 158
  experiences of 32, 52, 68, 93, 198
  filters 162–5
  during pandemic 158, 202–3
  pros and cons 157–9
  recommendations for managing
    165–7
  as saviour 158
  trends and censorship 159–62
Stonewall 151
stretchmarks 31, 147–50, 153, 201, 205
Strings, S. 127
Summers, Charl 31, 52, 73, 92, 112–13,
    186, 197
Switchboard LGBT+ 210

tattoos 178–82
thinness 14, 49, 90, 98, 125–6, 193
transgender men and women 104–5
transphobia 12, 41, 97, 139

Violet, Mia 29–30, 51–2, 74, 82–3, 85,
    91–2, 105–6, 112, 177–8, 187, 199
visibility 56, 140

Wade-Smith, Annie 31–2, 72, 112, 129,
    175, 185, 197
Waxman, O.B. 180
weight gain
  accepting 19, 132–5
  hostility towards 122, 124–5
  people commenting on 30, 114,
    132
weight loss 96, 100–1, 116, 132–3

worth
  based on attractiveness to cishet
    men 88, 115
  based on heteropatriarchal
    values 121
  bodily 67, 129, 137, 203, 206–7
  colonial standard of 155
  having confidence in 200

as person 21, 127–8
self-worth 61, 70, 194, 206–7
via capital 149
weight-health-worth paradigm
  130–2
'wrongness,' sense of 27–8, 29

Zucker, T. 95, 96